D1374123

Editing Texts of the Romantic Period

OTHER VOLUMES IN THIS SERIES

(*published by the University of Toronto Press*)

Editing Sixteenth-Century Texts edited by R. J. Schoeck

Editing Nineteenth-Century Texts edited by John M. Robson

Editing Eighteenth-Century Texts edited by D. I. B. Smith

Editor, Author, and Publisher edited by Wm. J. Howard

Editing Twentieth-Century Texts edited by Francess G. Halpenny

(*published by A. M. Hakkert Ltd.*)

Editing Seventeenth-Century Prose edited by D. I. B. Smith

Editing Texts
of the
Romantic Period

Papers given at the
Conference on Editorial Problems
University of Toronto,
November 1971

Edited by John D. Baird

Published for
The Committee for The Conference on Editorial Problems
by A. M. Hakkert Ltd., Toronto, 1972

Set in Aldine Roman by
A. M. Hakkert Ltd.

Printed and bound in Canada

Published for
The Committee for
The Conference on Editorial Problems
by
A. M. Hakkert Ltd.
554 Spadina Crescent
Toronto 179, Canada

Library of Congress Catalogue Card Number
72-96441

Standard Book Number
88866-522-9

Contents

Contributors

J. H. BURNS is Professor of the History of Political Thought and Head of the Department of History, University College London (England). Since 1961 he has been General Editor of The Collected Works of Jeremy Bentham.

KATHLEEN COBURN has recently retired from full-time teaching at Victoria College, University of Toronto. Her many publications include *Inquiring Spirit* (1951), *The Letters of Sara Hutchinson from 1800 to 1835* (1954) and *The Notebooks of Samuel Taylor Coleridge* (in progress). She is General Editor of The Collected Works of Samuel Taylor Coleridge.

W. J. B. OWEN is the author of *Wordsworth as Critic* (1969) and editor of *Wordsworth's Preface to Lyrical Ballads* (1957) and Wordsworth and Coleridge, *Lyrical Ballads, 1798* (1967). Mr. Owen, who is now engaged in editing the prose writings of Wordsworth, is Professor of English at McMaster University.

DONALD H. REIMAN is Editor of *Shelley and his Circle* at the Carl H. Pforzheimer Library, New York. Dr. Reiman's publications include *Shelley's The Triumph of Life: A Critical Study* (1965) and a general introduction to Shelley.

GEORGE WHALLEY is James Cappon Professor of English at Queen's University. His earlier works include *Poetic Process* (1953), *Coleridge and Sara Hutchinson* (1955), and *The Legend of John Hornby* (1962). He is presently completing his edition of Coleridge's marginalia for the "Collected Coleridge."

Editing Texts of the Romantic Period

Introduction

John D. Baird

In his introduction to the collection of papers given at the 1966 Conference on Editorial Problems, on editing nineteenth-century texts, John M. Robson forecast that the problems posed by texts of the Romantic period would shortly be the subject of another such Conference. However, as is the way in human affairs, other interests claimed prior attention, and five years passed before, on November 5 and 6, 1971, the seventh Conference in the series was convened on the University of Toronto campus to hear and discuss five papers on editing texts of the Romantic period. It was well attended; the presence of some sixty-five scholars from Canada and the United States, and a heartening number of graduate students from nearby universities, attested the widespread contemporary interest in the Romantics, and in the importance of good editions of their works.

The choice of 1971 as the year for this Conference had

* Members of the Committee for the 1971 Conference were: John D. Baird (Convener); G. E. Bentley, Jr.; A. H. de Quehen; David G. Esplin; Francess G. Halpenny; J. A. McClelland; John M. Robson.

one unlooked-for if minor advantage. We were spared
identification with either the Wordsworth bicentenary of
1970 or the Coleridge bicentenary of 1972. Both authors
are represented in the papers given here, and if Coleridge
appears twice to his old friend's once, that is a testimony
to the intricacy and variety of the editorial problems he
presents, rather than an expression of literary preference.
The northern shore of Lake Ontario has proved hospitable
to Coleridge studies, and the collection of MSS and early
editions at Victoria College of the University of Toronto is
the finest in North America. An exhibition of notable
items from this collection was on display in the E. J. Pratt
Library on the College campus during the Conference; an
appropriate tribute to Miss Coburn.

It is in the nature of the case that Miss Coburn's and
Professor Whalley's papers should be descriptive rather
than analytical, and the same is true of "The Bentham
Project" by J. H. Burns. Professor Burns (who little short
of miraculously evaded a strike of ground-crew at London
Airport in order to be with us) makes it clear that he too
faces problems of collecting and organizing huge quantities
of manuscript material; he, too, has awesome difficulties
to overcome in presenting such material in print. Both
Bentham and Coleridge, different though they were in so
many ways, aimed at comprehensiveness in their systems;
it was perhaps inevitable that their systems should have
remained incomplete. Both wrote voluminously, both
published a number of works, if but a fraction of what
they intended; yet both, so obstinately attached to their
writing desks, exerted their influence on the nineteenth
century primarily through personal contacts; almost, one
might say, through their disciples. Posthumous editions, of
one kind or another, were put out by Coleridge's family or
executors, and by Bentham's executor Bowring, but there
is a sense in which the nineteenth century did not need
learned editions; the thought and spirit of these great men
lived on in those who had known them personally. It was
left to our own more sceptical and intellectually frag-

mented age to restore the *disjecta membra*.

Bentham might rank poetry on the same low level with shove-halfpenny, but posterity has not endorsed that judgment, and we remember the great Romantics, rightly, as poets first and unacknowledged legislators of mankind second. Yet, even so, they have not always been well served by modern editors. Donald H. Reiman demonstrates this in his essay "Editing Shelley," and makes some detailed suggestions as to how the record may be improved. He is concerned, inevitably, with specifics, but it is worth stepping back for a moment to inquire how the situation he analyses has developed.

It is not always sufficiently recognized in the literary histories that the so-called reaction against Victorianism, associated with such names as Lytton Strachey, ran far deeper than a mere revolt against one's father's standards of literature and morality. The whole nineteenth century was under suspicion. (Much of the later Victorian sensibility was, of course, a legacy from the Romantics; even as many features of Victorianism, we are now aware, were current long before 1837.) Not least among the qualities of the Romantics to appear distasteful, especially after the First World War, was the magnanimity, the high idealism, the large and comprehensive expression of hope and goodwill for all the world (exact definition is elusive) which is found in one form or another in all the great English Romantics. This grudging attitude was summed up in the remark, reported to me by an Oxonian friend, made by an eminent Cambridge don giving a lecture in Oxford. He began to read from a poem of Shelley's (my informant had forgotten which), then broke off with the words: "I just can't go on with this; it's so *juvenile.*"

Nobody, to my knowledge, has attempted to study systematically the effect of literary taste on the undertaking of editions, or conversely, the effect of published editions on literary taste. Failing such a study, we can only pose questions. Was Grierson or Eliot the more important in restoring the Metaphysicals to favour? For restored they

were. I have before me a recently published volume in the
"Oxford English Texts" series. In the list of the series on
the dust-jacket, twenty-four poets are named; of these,
twelve are from the seventeenth century, and of these,
nine are commonly reckoned "Metaphysical." Coleridge,
Keats, and Wordsworth are there too, but the predomi-
nance of the seventeenth century is significant. In light of
this, we should not be surprised that interest in the
Romantics has only relatively recently begun to recover
from something of a slump; like an enthusiast for the
Metaphysicals in 1900, we shall not always find an
adequate text to hand. However, the situation is
improving. The impressive contemporary interest in Coleridge encourages and draws strength from the "Collected
Coleridge," and the same is true in different degrees of the
others. Because there are readers, editors are coming
forward; because there are editions, readership is growing.
Let us hope that all would-be editors in the field will heed
Dr. Reiman's strictures.

Editors in all fields would do well to heed Professor
Owen. His subject is Wordsworth, but his recommenda-
tions apply universally. Reading this paper, one is struck
again by the paradox of editing which Housman never
ceased to expound: the principles are simple, straightforward, self-evidently reasonable; yet they are seldom
consistently applied. Faced with this evidence of a fallen
world, we must resist despair, and arm ourselves instead
with the hope (appropriately Romantic emotion) that this
small volume will encourage and instruct all those who
undertake the duty of an editor.

* * * * * *

The Committee for the Conference on Editorial Problems wishes to record its gratitude to the Canada Council,
whose generous aid and interest is a great assistance, and to
the University of Toronto, for support continued even in
these days of stringency.

Editing the Coleridge Notebooks

Kathleen Coburn

There is a precedent for discussing problems connected
with the Coleridge notebooks after dinner. A crucial
conversation took place in such circumstances on the
terrace of The Chanter's House in Ottery St. Mary in 1936.
It involved Geoffrey Lord Coleridge's permission to
borrow and have photographed the 123 pages in Notebook
25 that contained Coleridge's notes for his Philosophical
Lectures. The photographing of those pages led to the
photographing of all the rest, without which the editing
would have been impossible. But that is a long story and I
take it that I am not put here in my anecdotage to try to
entertain you with an after-dinner speech, but to tell you
something of the problems of editing Coleridge, particularly the notebooks. It is tempting to pull the plums out of
them, and quote Coleridge on everything under the sun,
but there would be no end, and I believe I am supposed to
talk about much drier matters — having to do with
problems and methods. I shall not guarantee, however, to
abstain totally from the occasional tipple of Coleridge
himself.

The *Coleridge Notebooks* will run to five volumes, and

we are now into the proofs of Volume III.[1] There are some special problems in a multi-volume work, and perhaps because the material is Coleridge's, they vary somewhat from volume to volume. But from first to last in all of them, whatever the technical problems, for me as for Dr. Johnson, what really matters is the TEXT; annotation is always subordinate and has come to count for less and less.

The text of the Coleridge notebooks, as I have already described it in a general way in the Introduction to Volume I, is a chaos, in fact is a chaos made up of about 70 chaoses. I am not just being vague about the precise number of notebooks; I am being deliberately non-committal. Lowes discussed one small notebook, known as the Gutch Memorandum Book, in the British Museum. Lord Coleridge's collection from Ottery St. Mary added 55 to this. There are two in the Berg Collection in New York, plus one that may hardly be defined as a notebook — it is largely filled with a transcription in Watson's hand of the *Essay on Faith*. Something called by the late Alice Snyder, "The Bristol Notebook," which she published in *Coleridge on Logic and Learning*, is not properly speaking a notebook like any of the others. It contains in the hand of some amanuensis or transcriber about thirty-five pages on Logic; on the back and front pages are three brief memoranda in Coleridge's hand. It will be printed somewhere in the *Collected Works*. From the Leatherhead collection of the Rev. G. H. B. Coleridge (where Miss Snyder saw this "Bristol Notebook," now catalogued in Victoria College Library as B[ound] T[ranscript] 16, and the "Folio Notebook," now in the Huntington Library), we have the Victoria College Collection which includes Notebooks K, L, M, N, O, P and 56-65 (with three gaps), thirteen all told. That is if we are to call them all "notebooks."

I should explain perhaps the reason why some note-

1. Of *The Notebooks of Samuel Taylor Coleridge* (hereafter *CN*), two double volumes have appeared to date: I (1794-1804), New York, Pantheon, 1957; II (1804-1808), 1961. Volume III is expected early in 1973.

books are referred to by number, some by letters. All the Ottery St. Mary ones (bought by Lord Coleridge, the Lord Chief Justice, from his cousin Ernest Hartley Coleridge) bore home-made labels with numbers from 1-55 (again with gaps and some half-numbers, 3 1/2, 5 1/2, 21 1/2). Some of the Leatherhead ones (handed down from E. H. Coleridge to his son the Rev. G. H. B., to his son Mr. A. H. B. Coleridge) had similar labels and a few had numbers. One had the letter L in Coleridge's hand on the cover, so that it seemed to make sense to assign letters to the others and to avoid introducing yet another confusion by trying to number them into the numbered series. Not that the numbering is really serial in any true sense.

One thick notebook in the Berg Collection has a story connected with its number. It has always been known in the Berg Collection as the Clasped Vellum Notebook, and is so catalogued. Examination reveals, however, the round brown stain of a label removed, and the ever so faint traces of the number "29." That one is not imagining the number is proved by E. H. Coleridge's edition of the *Poetical Works* (II.1110) where in a note in an Appendix referring to the poem *Work without Hope* he quoted a large chunk from "Notebook No. 29, p. 168." This is an entry of 1825 and will appear in *CN* Volume IV, but for the present it leaves us in no doubt that N.29 was once with the rest. The reference also supports private information given some years ago that some time about 1910-12 the Coleridges suffered depradations at the hands of a book-thief butler who was caught and sentenced, but whose loot was never recovered. Books and MSS apparently passed through several hands and after a very smooth news column in *The Times* in 1930, they were finally offered in New York by the late Gabriel Wells. In 1943 the collection was bought for the Ham Collection and has been in the Berg since 1944.

This sort of thing, if given too much thought, makes one quake in the editorial shoes. Suppose other notebooks should turn up now?

And what is a notebook? Anything that was so numbered — ? — including the eight, scrappy bits about 3 1/2" x 4 1/2", pinned together as N° 65, called by Coleridge himself, "this Scrap-book"? And N°s 60 and 61, pages about 2 1/2" x 4 1/2" sewn together with someone's crochet cotton? And what of the Folio Notebook — at the other end of the scale — nearly 200 pages, 7" x 11 1/2"? The only satisfying policy is, perhaps, when in doubt, include. But is it the right one? Nineteenth century editors left us with all the frustrations of their exclusions. Perhaps we are now swinging to the other extreme. But that is how it is. Had I listened to one advisor, in the 1930s, the notebooks would have been published selectively, and I should have been spared a lot of hard work and a good deal of enlightenment. The most scrappy, unyielding little phrases, at first sight meaningless to anyone but the note-jotter himself, are sometimes the especially rewarding ones.

THE TEXT ITSELF

How far does one try to reproduce the writer's *intention*, how far try to reproduce what he actually wrote? How much can one do in the text? When I began, my inclination was towards common-sense modification, in the interests of a readable and sensible text that Coleridge might have printed — no Bowdlerizing, naturally, but silent corrections of some indifferent-seeming slips of the pen, slips in spelling when we know how Coleridge really did spell the word (no changes of his eighteenth- century habits certainly — like *compleatly* — or almost consistent eccentricities like his *knowlege* with no *d*, or *Edingburgh* with an extra *g*), but the occasional slip corrected and some minor punctuation supplied. I intended to preserve all "interesting" slips and revisions and to show, by pointed brackets (as I now in fact do), words or phrases that appeared to be later insertions or even casual afterthoughts. This common sense standard, sharpened a little by some awareness of the psychologically significant, was generally supported in the 1930s by those more experienced editors I consulted.

But when it came to applying what seemed to me common sense to Coleridge's vagaries, there was constant running war with my publisher's reader. In checking together some pages of my typescript against the photographs of the notebooks, we found ourselves disagreeing a dozen times a page. His common sense was very different from mine. At this rate the notebooks would never be published and I would collapse from nervous exhaustion and bad temper. The climax came one hot summer day over Coleridge's apostrophe *s*'s. Coleridge frequently (not always) writes as possessive of *it*, *it's*, the spelling now reserved for a contraction of *it is*, but sometimes he wrote *its'*. And when he wrote "Wordsworth's coat," let us say, where I had a normal *'s*, my reader could demonstrate with a compass and a ruler set to true north, that the apostrophe was east (or to the right) and not west (or to the left) of the final *s*. Now in order to save time and mounting blood pressure over all the apostrophe *'s* in a manuscript running to well over a million words, as well as over all the countless other minor problems of the same kind which you will readily envisage, I said we would standardize the apostrophe *s* and say so in the Introduction; we would retain Coleridge's punctuation otherwise, except in half a dozen instances which could be dealt with in notes; retain his spellings, all slips, insertions etc. In fact we would intrude on the text almost not at all. For one illegible word, we would use three dots, one dot each for each additional unread word (so far as one can guess at the number when unable to read them) up to ten dots, that is, eight unread words. The dots cheat on the resolve not to intrude, of course: and I have one or two other little ways of cheating where the difference between MS and type is such as positively to blind the reader to what is meant, but on the whole, we have approached as near as possible — and absolutely is not possible — to a facsimile in print. I have come to see real value in this. First of all there is the reader's confidence that things are not being tampered with, if he trusts his editor at all. While some helps to the reader (completion of words in square brackets, for example) and some helps to the editor, like *sic* — yet *sic* is a nuisance too — are removed, at the same time some misjudgments by the editor are avoided. There is the advantage too, that the reader is constantly reminded that this material is rough and unfinished. I still hope to prepare, some day, a nice readable *selection* from the notebooks, a good bedside book that will let you go to sleep over it, without alerting you constantly to revisions and pointed brackets and dotty passages. After all, scholarship has its responsibility to "the common reader" as well as to the text and the student. For this first time of presenting the highly complicated MS of the notebooks, an attempt at scholarly impeccability, however lacking in courage, is the essential course. Only after that, when we have learned all we can, should the modifications for readability be indulged in.

The retention of cancelled words and passages is an irritant to some readers; perhaps the following is a fair instance of the value of retaining them. In *CN* I.781, "that Torrent Crag opposite our ("our" possibly deleted, possibly not) Elderscat" was the first galley reading. It is a Keswick entry, and neither the late A. P. Rossiter nor I could read anything else, nor could we find such a place as "Elderscat," except that he didn't believe in my reading "our" and insisted that if it ever had been there it had been deleted and should be omitted as idiotic. "Elderscat" must be a local word, or an old name no longer used. What could "our" Elderscat be? Something to do with our elders' cat, or the cats of Greta Hall, on which consult Robert Southey perhaps? I am a firm believer in leaving what one sees in the text until the very last revised proofs — however idiotic — until one forces oneself to find the sense. Looking at the MS for the fiftieth time I suddenly saw — what seems so easy now — that it could read "Elder seat," two words, and the *our* was needed, and if it had been deleted in the galleys, the final page-proof reading would have looked less unlikely and might have slipped by unheeded; the reading was, "that Torrent Crag opposite our elder seat," i.e. the bench under the elder tree or bushes in the garden of Greta Hall, overlooking that once magnificent view, now all rooftops, towards the great Crag opposite.

I am convinced that errors and eccentricities should be preserved in the first printing of a MS, at least in a MS of this kind. Errors may be Coleridge's and of personal interest, or they may lead us to his sources. It is very inconvenient to have his Greek accented and corrected (as Professor Griggs and Miss Brinkley have done) for thereby one of the ways of telling whether Coleridge is writing out of his head or from a printed book is lost. *All* doubtful readings, too, are valuable, better than a guess or an omission that may distort interpretation for 150 years. E. H. Coleridge was an admirable editor and tackled gigantic tasks. Minor differences apart, my one very occasional quarrel with him is that he sometimes gave up too soon and silently omitted what was difficult to read. No MS of Samuel Taylor Coleridge is without its uncertainties. Besides, as I have said, a less than smooth formal text is a constant reminder to reader and editor (a) that we are prying into private papers that were never intended for us, and (b) that sometimes interpretation must be respectfully cautious, as for example in *CN* II.3045, an enciphered note where he is describing half-waking half-sleeping sensations. (It may be that the first part of this entry was cut away with the lower half of *f1ᵛ*). The cipher reads:

> Thought becomes a thing when it acts at once on your more [? conscious / consciousness] i.e. [? conscience/conscientiousness] therefore I dread to tell my whole & true case it seems to make a substantial reality/ I want it to remain a thought in which I may be deceived whole [?wholly]

The questions here are whether Coleridge is in fact

equating "consciousness" with "conscience" or
"conscientiousness" — or, reading "conscious conscience"
is there an implication of the possibility of an unconscious
conscience? A question with such very wide implications
should not be settled by any editorial plumping for one or
other reading. As to the last word in the entry, which is
followed by no punctuation, is the sentence complete, in
which case *wholly* would be the reading? Or is it not, in
which case, what was the intended continuation? It is also
necessary to know that the true beginning of the entry
may be missing — part of the page having been cut off
above it.

READINGS

A word about another kind of editorial conflict about
the text. The temptation to read what is reasonable,
instead of what is there, besets everyone, even the most
experienced, and with Coleridge it is never safe to accept
the reasonable possible against the irrational actual. For
instance, in Entry 1227, that is part of his Scawfell Tour
of 1802, Coleridge refers to a scholar in the Lakes who
teaches "a *lile lock* of Bairns" and though there are no
quotation marks — quotation marks are sparsely used in
the notebooks — the words appear to be reported speech.
My indefatigable adviser on the Lake country entries, A. P.
Rossiter, whose assiduity and high standards of accuracy
can hardly be exaggerated, read this phrase as "a lile *flock*
of Bairns." There is a little preceding vagueness with the
pencil which he took to be the letter *f*. It is a simple
reading and seems right. Yet I could not read it as *f*,
however hard I tried to make it into that reasonable word
flock. Occupied by the tussle with the MS, and focussing
on that aspect of the problem, we did not at once think of
what one should *always* at once think of, the *OED* and the
dialect dictionaries. The word *lock* in Cumberland and
Westmoreland is said to mean a handful, e.g. of hay, oats,
or such like. So, "a lile lock of bairns" is the reading, in
this light a much more charming phrase, "a handful of

bairns" rather than a "flock of bairns," besides being an indication, of which there are others, that Coleridge enjoyed the dialect speech of the north; as a Devon man he found it strange to his ears. Another odd reading, at first meaningless to us, in entry 797, was *Mungrane Bowscale*. It could be found on no map of any period, not even on the map in Hutchinson's *History of Cumberland* which (Notebook 2 proves) Coleridge used for his explorations. We tried to read it every sort of way: Mungrane Bowscale it insisted on being. From his route it had to be near or in Mungrisedale. But persistence revealed to Rossiter that the English Place Names Society, in its volume on Cumberland and Westmorland, described in some detail its doubts and difficulties about a place called Mungrane, referred to in the year 1589, but only dubiously thought to be connected with Mungrisedale. Coleridge's reference to it here, in conjunction with Bowscale close by, clears up the whole uncertainty. The Place Names volume corroborated our reading, and our reading fills in a small gap in their information about the historical and geographical reality and location of Mungrane.

Some correct readings come by chance as a hair-raising experience at the last moment: for example, "Miss W. lamed" written in very faint clumsy pencil on the edge of a very small page, became in the final page proofs at the eleventh hour, after I had chased Dorothy Wordsworth all over the Lakes trying to catch her spraining her ankle, thanks to a shaft of sunlight in the MS Room of the British Museum, not "Miss W. lamed" but "My spirits tamed."

SEQUENCE AND CHRONOLOGY

The problem in *CN* I was the decision as to method of presentation, and it was really owing to an argument with Lawrence Hanson — whose sensitive first volume of an uncompleted biography appeared in 1934 — that I found it necessary to work out the present system of enumerating entries within each notebook and then in a chronological

series. Hanson argued that he and others like him wished
to know what was before and after and opposite any given
entry — and urged publication of the notebooks as they
stand, one by one, page by page. But this was impractical
on various counts. For one, Coleridge did not write in his
notebooks page after page, but sometimes back to front,
middle to back, middle to front, and sideways. Short of
photographic reproduction it would have been impossible
to show the physical juxtapositions. Notebook 22, for
instance, is five or six notebooks or gatherings inserted one
inside the other. For another, it would have meant a
turning out of a time-chaos without the clues or hints
conveyed in the original by changes of ink, slope of the
hand, spacing, and so on. So it made sense to agree with
Coleridge himself when he said ". . . the chronological
order is the best for arranging a poet's works. All your
divisions are in particular instances inadequate, and they
destroy the interest which arises from watching the
progress, maturity, and even the decay of genius." (*Table
Talk*; 1 January 1834.) But by numbering the entries in
each notebook according to position, and then superim-
posing on these a chronological serial order, it became
possible to show both the contiguities within each notebook, and the calendar of the writing. Roughly.

Next to reading the words themselves, sometimes in fact
even more difficult than the deciphering (in spite of E. K.
Chambers saying the notebooks were illegible), is the
conveying exactly what one wishes to convey about dates
and the chronological order. Take one of the simpler cases:
N 3, where the 53 entries begin in September 1798 and
run through October, and into 1799, probably to 30 June
1799. Other notebooks used in this period are N 3 1/2,
and N 21. (I have chosen one of the most straightforward
early periods.) But what is one to do in serializing
chronologically with two entries not datable any more
closely than October 1798 - February 1799, or one c. June
- December 1799, or one 1798 - 23 April 1799? Or what
do I do with an entry (N 3 1/2) datable only as

1799-1803? That there are other spans of possibility much wider can be seen by looking at the tables in the back of the *CN* volumes. Coleridge himself exclaims, with a series of exclamation marks, "Twenty-three years between the entries on this page!" His own dates are generally correct, sometimes wrong in the day of the week, or out by one day; but one must be a bit cautious in accepting all the dates as his, for Mrs. Gillman's hand appears from time to time with an "Alas! Alas!" and, one suspects, a date or two. For instance, I am raising a question in *CN* III about T. M. Raysor's acceptance of an 1808 date for some lecture material; it may be Mrs. Gillman's 1808 and the lecture notes could be for the 1811-12 series — but all this is more by way of question than answer.

Another difficulty in making the dating clear comes from the fixity of print. A chronological series is naturally assumed to be truly chronological, utter what caveats one may against believing in it too rigidly. There the entries are, in position, in sequence. Yet entries are sometimes datable by month only (usually put at the end of the month; by the year only at the end of the year), but if they are in a run of entries some of which are more specifically datable in that month/year, should one pull out the specifically dated, for the sake of a system? Say for example in N X of 50 entries, X.1, 15, 40 and 45 are dated January 2, 22, 25, February 10 respectively. The others show no evidence of any date other than January/February 1800. In such a case I have left the normal notebook sequence undisturbed — unless there is some good reason to suppose a break in use of the notebook. But a break can be the break of an hour or two — or of 23 years — it is not possible to tell.

This problem worries an editor perhaps more than it bothers readers. (Perhaps we only want them to bother more.) In the end one has to rely, in the cruxes, on the reader using the table at the back of the book. If someone would invent a fount of type that could *squeak*, I should every few pages have it squeaking, "Don't trust me too far!"

"SOURCES" ANNOTATION

Reading the MS to arrive at the correct text and tracing
to sources are often interdependent operations, as we all
know, and, as I say, sometimes the answers come by mere
chance. I do not know what good it does to anyone to talk
about the importance of chance in such work, unless it be
to recommend serendipity as a kind of tranquillizer. If an
entry is very faint, or much scribbled over, or badly written − say, written in a jolting stage coach with a stubby
pencil in the bottom sixteenth of an inch of the page of a
small pocket book − knowledge of a printed source may
make it possible − without cheating − to read what was
badly written.

The late Mr. Humphry House and I lamented all one
summer about not being able to find *CN* I.1075:

> So many earles & viscounts, that it were long to rehearse − it
> was a great beauty to behold the Banners & Standardes waving
> in the Wind, & horses barded & squires richly armed.

He had quoted it in the Clark Lectures that he was preparing for the press and he was doubtful about his transcription, and I about mine, and we differed from each
other in some readings. The particularly difficult words
were *barded*, and *standardes*. It was clearly an excerpt
from a medieval work − or from some work quoting a
medieval work − but there was no clue from surrounding
entries. (What preceded was six lines of German verse
[Schiller's] and what followed was a reflection on the
effect of opium on breathing.) One evening, in pursuit of a
quotation Coleridge said was from Francis Bacon, which
proved incidentally to be from Sir John Stewart in *Political Economy*, I reached to a shelf for a volume of the
Advancement of Learning. Now my father in his early days
as a country parson was the victim of a good many college
boys selling books in their summers, and from one of these
he bought a set called "The World's Greatest Literature."
If any of you know these cheap, tactually loathsome volumes, you know that their publishers must have been of

that order of men who think, of books and women, that
sterling character does not go with a pleasing exterior. On
a dull binding they printed in faint very perishable virginal
white the titles of the world's greatest masterpieces. Most
of the titles have gone entirely. The result for me was that,
from one of a few of these volumes purloined from the
family set, I took down not Bacon's *Advancement of
Learning* as I intended, but Froissart's *Chronicles of England, France and Spain*. Beginning to read, witlessly where
it opened, something electric distracted me at once from
my interest in *The Advancement of Learning*; for even in
the dull flat translation of Thomas Johnes I knew I was
reading the work from which CN I.1075 must have come.
It was fifteen minutes to closing time of the main library,
and the thermometer I recall was at 10° below zero, but I
made it in time to get out the translation Coleridge rel-
ished, the old one of Sir John Bourchier, Lord Berners.
Coleridge's exact words were there, in Chapter 41, though
he had modernized the spelling. I did not have to go to bed
that night in a state of unbearable excitement and curiosity. (After all, this thing had been eluding me for about 15
years or more.) The correct reading came, too late alas, for
Humphry House's book, too late for him to know that our
finally agreed-on reading of *barded* was correct, and that
his *standards* had an *e* in it, which could be seen in Coleridge's holograph when one knew it was there in Lord
Berners text.

   It may be of little use to tell other hard-working editors
about miracles of this Froissart-for-Bacon kind. Yet aside
from the fact that perhaps some encouragement may be
derived from evidence that miracles in favour of mankind
do happen still, there may be also something else. The
foolish manual accident of the wrong volume would have
yielded nothing had I not long been looking hard for that
snippet — and not once, but several times. The pale translation of Johnes of this passage reads: "I must say, it was a
fine thing to see and reflect upon; for there were banners
and pennons flying, and the richest armor on both sides."

Compare the 1075 reading above. Only someone whose subconscious had been for a long time subjected to Coleridge's entry would, I think, have had this link subterraneously forged for him. I am appalled to realise how many of such connexions must be missed when we are hell-bent on some irrelevancy like Bacon, and the *Advancement of Learning*. The consolation is, that fruitless-seeming searches are not altogether fruitless. Perhaps another moral is (but this is a matter of temperament), it's no good consulting the experts too soon. I like to have beaten around all my own bushes before I do so, because things turn up unexpectedly, things you are not looking for, things that the experts cannot notice as relevant.

ANNOTATION

I am not saying much about annotating. There are few generalizations to be made about it. Every work, author, type of MS, presents its own unique problems. Works published by the author and meant to make sense to readers require for the most part but terse references to sources, identification of persons, causes, obsolete events or words, perhaps a few cross-references where further illumination of a point can be had this way. Letters, on the other hand, though intended to make sense to one person or a group of persons, can be enriched by a little more explanation of personal allusions, shared tastes, jokes, and so on. Literary allusions it seems to me should be clarified always and, in Coleridge's case, his reading being so wide and so intense, with all possible attention to editions, reviews in periodicals, and so on. Marginalia are a different game again, Samuel Taylor Coleridge in dialogue with an author (his favourite kind of dialogue of course, where the other party is mum — for the moment at least), blackening his margins. George Whalley will have something to say about the subtleties of notes on notes. Notebooks — if I may say so in extenuation of my own sometimes very long notes — are the most private incommunicative form of writing, leaving the largest areas to be mapped. Sometimes behind the briefest jotting lies a whole world of unknowns – as John Livingston Lowes discovered. (After all, he wrote a work of over 600 pages on one small notebook of 303 entries – two pages an entry; my record does not approach that.) I do sometimes pine for the classical style of reference, indicative merely, without descriptions of the MS, the state of the holograph, the uncertainties of dating, even the doubts about readings, let alone the questions of doubtful meanings, possible relationships or Coleridge's various uses of an entry. But in fact, the shorter the entry, very often the longer the note needed to discuss it. The more hidden the relevant facts, the more long-winded the race to find them, and need to show from various possibilities which is the likeliest path to the truth about them. I know I have erred on the side of what Coleridge believed in – "fuller explanations and a less asserting tone." But at least we have put the notes in a separate volume where you may ignore them completely. At your peril!

BY INDIRECTION FIND DIRECTION OUT

I am afraid my attempt to comment on the problems of editing the Coleridge notebooks is rather more defense and apology than a series of helpful hints. But if there is one small tip that we sometimes learn the hard way, and it may or may not apply so frequently to other nineteenth-century authors, it is that when searching for the meaning of a passage, or the source of a reference or quotation, we save time by looking first in our man himself. Coleridge is, I suppose, next to Milton, perhaps the widest reader among English writers. With a good memory, he was a meditative reader who chewed over in all sorts of contexts the thoughts that his reading provoked, extrapolating from it. Therefore in order to catch Coleridge's thought on the wing it is necessary to read everything he ever wrote. Lowes hunted fruitlessly for years for a reference he wanted by Coleridge to the Wandering Jew; he did not think of looking for it in the marginalia in the eighth volume of Tennemann's *Geschichte der Philosophie* – and who would blame him? I have sometimes been shaken at the page proof stage, by stumbling upon the elucidation of some joke, or the simple solution of some heavily-weathered problem, right under my nose in some Coleridge letter, printed work, or MS fragment. So if Coleridge refers some phrase to Aquinas or Erasmus, I know by now that it is folly to go first to the great folios of those writers; one must go to other places where he talks about them, discover if possible which of their works he read, if possible in which edition. One must more often than not by indirection find direction out.

It is for this reason that an edition of all Coleridge writings, letters, marginalia, notebooks, and all the published and unpublished works down to the smallest fragment, is needed, and that indexes are an important part of such work. This is why we are so fortunate that the Bollingen Foundation, before it folded its tents, decided to embark with Rupert Hart-Davis on the Collected Works. (It may seem – looking at the history of Coleridge's printers and publishers, from the printer of *The Friend* [who took to the bottle] to Gale & Curtis and Rest Fenner [the last two of whom took to their heels and the U.S.] to the Pilot Press [which sank under the *Philosophical Lectures*] to Hart-Davis and Bollingen [needless to say, in quite other categories] – that Coleridge had a way of breaking the camel's back, and one wonders at times about the editorial backs.) But perhaps you will permit a few words more – about the Collected Coleridge.

COLLECTED COLERIDGE

When the vast quantity of unpublished material is published, marginalia, fragments of MSS, and notebooks, we shall see, if not a new Coleridge, new sides of him, or at least we shall, I think, attach more importance to some new aspects of his prose works already published and largely unread.

In the first place, when his editors after his death came to consider publication of his manuscript remains, they

were confronted with a colossal problem, in sheer physical
bulk alone. In choosing what to publish and what not to
publish, they thought of what they, in the 1830s, '40s, and
'50s considered important, either as conducive to Coleridge's and the family's reputation, or to the dissemination
of what in their own view was *the* sound faith, political,
religious, philosophical, or literary. They wanted to offset
Cottle's *Recollections* and *Reminiscences* — ungentle-
manly, they charged (in private correspondence). Cottle
publicly spilled the beans about the opium, and perhaps
understandably displayed his own generosity and STC's
financial ineptitude. Besides, for most of the Victorian
Coleridges, truth was Tory and Church of England. They
had no notion of STC's psychological insights; and his philosophical editor was, it must be said, Green in more than
name. Even their relish for the literary materials was, shall
we say, less catholic than STC's own. Like others in the
Victorian era, they were strong on moral improvement by
means of literature. Moreover, by publishing their great
ancestor's works selectively they could kill two birds at
once; they could give the lie to those who attacked Coleridge's career and character by charging him with moral
irresponsibility — it was a live issue in the two decades
after his death — and they could preach the true gospel as
they saw it. Their labours were immense, and their piety
heroic. All honour to them, but they were often limited
and sometimes just wrong. Sara Coleridge was probably
the most learned of her father's editors; and she is one who
cannot, so far as I know, be charged with tampering with
any text. She said in a letter to Aubrey de Vere that none
of the family understood her father fully. Her husband,
Henry Nelson Coleridge, Coleridge's nephew and son-in-
law, was accused by Hartley Coleridge and by Tom Poole
of having made him in the *Table Talk* more Tory than he
was and by Crabb Robinson of having made him too
goody-goody. H. N. Coleridge had been assigned the task
of editing the literary remains, Derwent the theological,
and J. H. Green, the official executor, took on himself the

philosophical documents. H. N. Coleridge died two years
after Coleridge, and much of what he did was based on
copying by paid transcribers; J. H. Green produced a
garbled interpretation of so-called "Spiritual Philosophy";
and Derwent, who did publish some interesting volues of
theological marginalia, was a harried college principal, not
always in agreement with his father; there are instances
where a nineteenth-century attitude to editing allowed him
to modify the text accordingly, even in one case to supply
a negative in a positive sentence.

All the same, if there has been some distortion of Coleridge the whole man and thinker, the slanted impressions
cannot all be attributed to his industrious family editors.
Some of them arose from his own fear of being misunder-
stood — hence the recurrent and confusing qualifications
and retractions — some of them from the timidity induced
by Big Brother (and he had nine of those).

The Routledge-Bollingen Edition of the *Collected Works*
— the financial administration and distribution is now in
Princeton — is presenting all the works, published and unpublished, according to clear principles established at the
beginning by Hart-Davis and Bollingen. Lectures to an
audience are separately treated as one kind of thing, prose
works seen through the press another, reported table talk
another, marginalia on books another, and MSS fragments
another. The divisions are not made according to subject
matter, as, for example, in *Shakespearean Criticism*, but
according to the form of communication. There were
different audiences in mind and different incentives for
each kind of writing. Newspaper pieces will be in two volumes, marginalia in four or five, literary lectures in two,
the all but unknown *Logic* in one, the *Table Talk* (con-
siderably larger than the original) in one, and so on.[2] The

2. The following volumes have been published, by Routledge and Kegan
Paul of London and the Princeton University Press: I. *Lectures 1795 on Poli-
tics and Religion*, eds. Lewis Patton and Peter Mann (1971); II. *The Watch-
man*, ed. Lewis Patton (1970); III and IV. *The Friend*, ed. Barbara Rooke
(1969); VI *Lay Sermons*, ed. R. J. White.

labour and expense – and the intellectual rewards to those who work on all this – are immense. We hope we are gathering a harvest almost as rich for others. It is not necessary to identify with or agree with one's author, if he is a truly great mind. I hope there will never be a Coleridge Society. Coleridge can do without idolaters. Editing begins in curiosity about and respect for one's author and for my part at least cannot be carried on without them. Surely one cannot have greater good fortune than to have been attracted early to a subject for which familiarity breeds only greater curiosity and increasing respect.

Editing Shelley

Donald H. Reiman

Shelley and his Circle is an unusual publication that does not attempt to be a complete edition of the letters or writings of any single author; it is a catalogue-edition of one library's collection of manuscripts centering on William Godwin, Shelley, Lord Byron, Leigh Hunt, and their friends and correspondents.[1] For those not familiar with our editorial procedures, let me outline them briefly. The manuscripts — the great majority of them holograph letters — appear in chronological order, as nearly as that can be determined. Each manuscript is introduced by a Bibliographical Description, which first describes the literary and the physical aspects in general terms — the number of pages of writing and the size of the pages — and then

1. *Shelley and his Circle*, published by Harvard University Press and Oxford University Press: Volumes I-II by Kenneth Neill Cameron, Editor, with Contributing Editors Eleanor L. Nicholes and Frederick L. Jones, 1961; Volumes III-IV by Kenneth Neill Cameron, Editor, with Contributing Editors Sir Gavin De Beer, David V. Erdman, Eleanor Flexner, Frederick L. Jones, and Sylva Norman, 1970; Volumes V-VI by Donald H. Reiman, Editor, with Coordinating Editor Doucet D. Fischer and Contributing Editors David V. Erdman, R. Glynn Grylls (Lady Rosalie Mander), Sylva Norman, and Marion Kingston Stocking, 1973.

enumerates the kind of paper (and its watermark and countermark, if any), the seal, the postal fee(s), the postmark(s), any dockets, notations, or additions (such as spindle holes or adhering pieces of paper or tape), and the provenance of the manuscript. Next there is a diplomatic Transcription of the text of the manuscript, with Textual Notes keyed to the Transcription by line number. There may be collations of other authoritative manuscripts or of printed texts. Finally there is a Commentary that attempts to elucidate all factual problems and literary and biographical implications of the letter, document, or literary text that are not discussed in another Commentary — its date, its biographical significance, the background of its references and allusions.

To provide broader contexts for these specific Commentaries, each major figure whose manuscripts appear in the series is introduced by a general essay on his life and works. Various other topics — biographical, bibliographical, and critical — are also given extended treatment in essays. The essays in Volumes V-VI, for example, are "Edward John Trelawny" (Life and Works); "Trelawny to Augusta White: Introduction to a Correspondence"; "The Composition and Publication of *The Revolt of Islam*"; "Keats and Shelley: Personal and Literary Relations"; "Claire Clairmont's Journal"; "Peacock in Leadenhall Street"; and "Shelley's Treatise on Political Economy." The late Carl H. Pforzheimer and Kenneth Neill Cameron conceived of the entire catalogue-edition as comprising an interlocking collective biography of William Godwin, Mary Wollstonecraft, Shelley, Mary Shelley, Thomas Love Peacock, Hunt, and Byron, up to the time of Shelley's death. This general aim continues (though we have extended the terminal date from 1822 to include the important Byron manuscripts that post-date Shelley's death). The volumes are focused to include an audience composed not only of literary scholars but of literate general readers as well. With this broader audience in mind, we avoid coding our footnote references by initials and in-group abbreviations, a practice that we hope will also help to keep the work readable after some of the currently fashionable abbreviations are *passé*.

Because all of the edited materials are taken directly from manuscripts that are on the premises, the editor and staff enjoy repeated opportunities to collate the typescript or the proofs of a text with the manuscript to ascertain the most probable readings and to comment on difficulties in textual notes. Having a large group of interrelated manuscripts greatly aids us also in dating letters and establishing their sequence. A letter, otherwise undatable, may be put within certain limits because the paper on which it is written is from the stock used by the writer only during a short period of time. We can more accurately date some letters because we have the dated postmarks on the letters to which they are answers, and we can date others because we know the post days in Italy and how long it took letters to travel from Italy to England, where they received a date-stamp from the Foreign Post Office. In the Commentaries, we attempt to extend the available information on minor figures, like Shelley's publisher Charles Ollier, by drawing together references from manuscripts and from obscure books that more general libraries or more specialized scholars, devoting themselves entirely to Shelley or another major figure, might not be aware of. Sometimes we are enabled to correct the text of Shelley's letters simply because we repeatedly encounter similar small problems. In three cases, for example, we found notations written on letters that were apparently in handwriting other than that of the author and that were difficult to connect with the context of their respective letters. One was a letter from Peacock to Charles Ollier, one from Shelley to Ollier, and one written by Mary Shelley in Shelley's name to Ollier. In the case of the two Shelley items, previous editors had included the notations as postscripts or notes in the text of the letters themselves. We finally concluded, however, after considering the position of the words, the similarity of the scrawled handwriting, and the common destination of the three letters, that the notations had been random notes jotted down by Charles or James Ollier while the letters in question were spindled on the desk in front of him. We were thus able to remove these irrelevant notes from the texts of the letters.

In addition to the opportunities afforded by the concentration of manuscripts in The Carl H. Pforzheimer Library, the format of *Shelley and his Circle* provides the editor with scope to pursue in detail topics that would necessarily be scanted in an edition that confined annotation to laconic footnotes. On a few topics at least, *Shelley and his Circle* may serve as a textbook for novice scholars. When we redate a letter, we outline the evidence on which we do so, providing other scholars not only with the material to judge the validity of the individual decision, but also with paradigms of arguments and types of evidence that they can apply to similar problems. Besides noting such customary details as literary and historical allusions, we delve into areas like publishing and printing techniques, the operation of the postal system, banking and business practices, relevant medical and legal information, and, in general, the web of daily affairs in the early nineteenth century that underlay the lives and literary works of the major figures.

For example, when analyzing the textual changes that Shelley made in December 1817 while transforming *Laon and Cythna* into *The Revolt of Islam*, I found it useful to discover that (1) incest was not a civil crime in England in Shelley's day — and therefore Shelley's depiction of incest in *Laon and Cythna* did not render the poem liable to prosecution on that account —, although (2) *Blackwood's Edinburgh Magazine* for November 1817 contained a fierce attack on Leigh Hunt's use of incest in *The Story of Rimini*. (3) The uncomplimentary references to Christianity were, on the other hand, *legally* dangerous, since a bookseller named James Williams of Portsea had just been convicted, fined, and imprisoned for republishing two

relatively innocent political tracts cast in the form of
religious parodies. Study of a tradesman's bill for Russia
oil has enabled us to elucidate the point of a contemporary
joke in *Peter Bell the Third*. And for writers of more
frequent contemporary allusiveness — like Byron in *Don
Juan* or Leigh Hunt and Thomas Moore in their journalistic
poetry and prose — such commentary on the methods and
manners of Regency England should prove useful not only
because of specific information that we provide but also
because we point other scholars toward particular books
and methods of research.

As an astute reviewer of Volumes III and IV of *Shelley
and his Circle* pointed out, one characteristic of the
research in the edition is that it raises almost as many
scholarly questions as are answered. Indeed, I think that it
is an important duty of any scholar not only to track
down particular information that has eluded his predeces-
sors, but also to raise new questions and problems that, if
solved by researchers in the future, will result in fuller
knowledge not only of the *actions* of poets but of their
unstated reasonings as well. The commentaries in the
forthcoming volumes of *Shelley and his Circle* probe into
Shelley's motivations, for example, in the dates he assigned
to the composition of his poems. Using varied evidence, I
reject the date conventionally agreed upon for the composition of *Julian and Maddalo*. I argue that Shelley, for
quite cogent and intelligible reasons, purposely misled
Leigh Hunt and Mary Shelley about the period in which
the poem was composed.

In short, though we begin with the physical evidence of
the manuscripts, leading to verbal and syntactical evidence
of the texts, our aims are larger. From the unvarnished
facts, we move first to biographical or bibliographical
evidence and finally to literary implications. By analyzing
closely three leaves of holograph fair copy of *Laon and
Cythna* in the Pforzheimer Library and using evidence
from their provenance and from the other scattered leaves
of fair copy, I was able to determine that the surviving

portion of fair copy of Canto IX actually contains the final text and served as press copy, whereas the surviving fair copy of Canto I (which previous commentators have assumed to be part of the same continuous manuscript) was actually an *intermediate* fair copy, which did *not* go to press. This conclusion on the one hand refutes those who have used the state of the fair copy of Canto I as evidence that Shelley did not take great pains in preparing his poem for the press and, on the other hand, coupled with analysis of the rough draft manuscripts in the Bodleian, it suggests that parts of Canto I were written either after or at the same time as the end of Canto XII. This inference, in turn, has critical implications by pointing up hitherto unnoted parallels between the symbolic voyages at the end of the first and twelfth cantos.

A cardinal principle that has guided us in editing *Shelley and his Circle* is the assumption that the author of the manuscript before us is correct until he has been proven in error. By searching diligently for first-class confirmatory evidence to document a reference or assertion, by checking contemporary dictionaries and rhetorics, as well as the *Oxford English Dictionary* to vindicate an unusual spelling or use of a word, by following technical terms (like "chariot" for a particular kind of coach or "Russia oil" for a specific hairdressing) into the technical manuals and even the magazine advertisements of the period, we have learned far more and added more to the stock of knowledge than would have been possible had we simply assumed that references and usages not found in standard reference works or earlier books on Shelley were either erroneous or insignificant.

One might suppose that the principle I have just stated — that the writer being edited is presumed to be correct until he has been proven to be in error — would be accepted by most modern scholars. Unfortunately, its acceptance by Shelley scholars does not appear to be at all unanimous. One can contrast Kenneth Neill Cameron's annotation of Shelley's letters in *Shelley and his Circle* with that of Frederick L. Jones in his *Letters of Percy Bysshe Shelley*.[2] Although Jones declares that he is publishing the text of Shelley's letters as faithfully as possible, he sometimes gives way to an urge to show his intellectual superiority to Shelley — usually with disastrous results. For example, when he corrects Shelley's "agua" to "acqua" in a foreign quotation, he has failed to notice that the quotation is Spanish, not Italian (II, 132). Another time he adds this note to the opening sentence of one of Shelley's letters: "The syntax of this sentence is confused: 'would have operated' appears to have no subject." In fact, the sentence — though complex — is grammatically and syntactically quite correct, the subject of the verb in question being a gerund ("your declining") which Jones must have read as a present participle (I, 578-579). The sentence reads: "It is to be regretted that you did not consult your own safety and advantage, if you consider it connected with the non-publication of my book, before your declining the publication, after having accepted it, would have operated to so extensive and serious an injury to my views as now."

When Shelley twice within a month writes to two publishers about "your announce of *Frankenstein*" (I, 564) and "the announce of *Laon & Cythna* in the public papers" (I, 568), Jones twice adds a bracketed suffix after Shelley's word, changing "announce" to "announce-[ment]." Why? A better course would have been to note that "though *announce* does not appear in the *Oxford English Dictionary*, Shelley is clearly coining the word on the analogy of the French '*annonce*' and Italian '*annuncio*.'" In fact, Shelley's usage is not wholly without contemporary parallel.[3]

---

2. Two volumes. Oxford, The Clarendon Press, 1964.

3. While reading periodical reviews of the time for my edition of contemporary reviews of the Romantic poets (*The Romantics Reviewed*, 9 vols., New York, Garland Publishing Inc., 1972), I came upon two analogous uses of the French form. Francis Jeffrey writes in his review of Wordsworth's *Poems, in Two Volumes* (1807): "... we read the *annonce* of Mr. Wordsworth's publications with a good deal of interest and expectation ..."

Using my marked copy of *The Letters of Percy Bysshe Shelley*, I could enumerate many similar instances in which Jones has provided information that is erroneous, often contradicting Shelley as he does so. But perhaps it would be more efficient to cite one epitomizing example of what happens when a scholar sets out to supplement or correct his author without devoting sufficient care or attention to his research. Jones's edition of Mary Shelley's letters contains an editorial blunder that I find dazzling. Mary Shelley writing to Maria Gisborne, discusses Jane Williams, and adds: "but I preach in vain – J–– C–– says 'Do unto others as you would they should do unto you.'" Jones, ever mindful of the ignorant reader, identifies the source of the quotation by expanding the initials "J. C." to "J[ohn] [Wheeler] C[leveland]," Jane Williams' brother.[4]

All editors make errors, and I do not mean to imply that Jones's work is below the usual standards of editions of the letters of nineteenth-century poets. Those who have followed the reactions to the Clarendon Press editions of Thomas Moore's letters and the letters of Dante Gabriel Rossetti will be aware that not all the work in this field has met the high standards set by the editors of the letters of Blake, Keats, and Swinburne. But the standards of competence exhibited in editions of the letters, poetry, and prose of nineteenth-century authors *must* rise above their present dead level if literary scholars, students, and literate readers are to appreciate fully the intelligence, wit, wisdom, and great aesthetic power of the major figures of the period. I am not calling for new theoretical break-throughs in the techniques of textual analysis; I am simply suggesting that, unless editors of literary texts of the nineteenth century learn the basic methods already

(*Edinburgh Review* 11, October, 1807, p. 215), and twelve years later a reviewer writes of Wordsworth's *Peter Bell* and *The Waggoner*: ". . . the pompous *annoncé* of these tales . . . seemed like the ushering of a washer-woman into a drawing room" (*Eclectic Review*, 2nd Series, 12, July, 1819, p. 63).

4. *Letters of Mary W. Shelley*, Norman, University of Oklahoma Press, 1944, II, 107-108.

employed in other areas of literary scholarship, the work of an entire generation of such scholars may turn out to be little more than a furious spinning of wheels.

For example, scholars of the Romantic period, in general, stand greatly in need of training in the analysis and use of manuscript evidence. No medievalist would think of editing an important text without studying paleography. No editor of Shakespeare or other Renaissance dramatists could work in ignorance of the principles of bibliographical analysis, and if he did, no respectable press would publish his efforts. Yet in nineteenth-century scholarship, edition after edition appears in which editors, apart from a general interest in writing criticism or studying the biography of a poet or novelist, demonstrate few qualifications for their principal task of producing a text as close to the author's intention as surviving evidence and human fallibility will permit.

For one thing, the editor of a work for which a full holograph manuscript survives ought to be able to determine whether the manuscript he has before him is a rough draft, an intermediate fair copy, the copy that went to press, or an extra transcript retained by the author. Obviously, if the manuscript was the one carefully prepared by the author to send to press, the manuscript ought to be used as copy text, especially if the author is known not to have revised proofs. Whereas, if the manuscript is either an intermediate fair copy or what we may term a "safe-keeping copy," it is not as authoritative on accidentals and may not be as authoritative on substantives as the text of the first edition. On the other hand, an intermediate fair copy often reveals much about the author's intentions when he revises, cancels, or inserts passages. These are simple truths. Yet texts of two works by the younger Romantics that have been most lavishly re-edited are fundamentally flawed because the editors failed to determine the nature and the implications of the manuscripts available to them.

I have written and spoken elsewhere about the limita-

tions of Lawrence John Zillman's two editions of Shelley's
Prometheus Unbound.[5] Let me say here only that Zillman's recent Yale Press edition uses Shelley's intermediate
fair copy in two illegitimate and harmful ways. First, he
introduces too many readings from it into the text of *Prometheus* against the authority of the first edition (which
was taken directly from the lost final copy prepared for
the press by Shelley and Mary Shelley). Second, Zillman
uses the wide divergence in many accidental features
between the first edition and the very unfinished fair copy
that survives to argue for and to practice a textual
relativism in which the editor's taste rather than objective
evidence becomes the factor determining which readings
will be given.

   Truman Guy Steffan began his textual study of Byron's
poetry years ago as co-editor with Willis W. Pratt of the
elaborate Variorum Edition of *Don Juan.* More recently he
has appeared as editor of *Lord Byron's "Cain."* Both of
these editions have their useful features, but when it comes
to the technical matter of determining textual authorities
and analyzing evidence from them, Steffan throws up his
hands in confusion and patches together a text as best he
can. Steffan speaks at length of "the MS of *Cain,*" and
even asks the question as to whether this manuscript
served as printer's copy. But he gives no answer, even
though the unsorted facts he supplies make it evident that
the manuscript is *not* the one that went to John Murray,
but Byron's intermediate fair copy, kept by him in Italy.
What happened to the press copy? Is it now in John
Murray's files in Albemarle Street? Does Steffan know? He
gives no indication of having written to ask. In any case,

   5. Lawrence John Zillman, ed., *Shelley's "Prometheus Unbound": A
Variorum Edition*, Seattle, University of Washington Press, 1959; Lawrence
John Zillman, ed., *Shelley's "Prometheus Unbound": The Text and the
Drafts*, New Haven, Yale University Press, 1968. The latter edition was
reviewed by Donald H. Reiman in *JEGP* 68, July 1969, pp. 539-543; both
editions were discussed by Donald H. Reiman in "Textual and Aesthetic
Problems in Shelley's *Prometheus Unbound*," a paper delivered to the
Bibliographical Evidence group of the Modern Language Association of
America, 28 December 1969, at Denver, Colorado.

without seeing anything except the manuscript before him at Texas, Steffan should have known that it had not received Byron's final polishing and that it therefore has limited usefulness as a textual authority. But Steffan does not reach this logical conclusion: instead he, like Zillman, falls back on personal taste. Though properly taking the first edition as his copy text, Steffan adds: "There are a few deviations in words from the 1821 text, and on these occasions I used the MS version, because it seemed preferable" (p. 147). All in all, *Lord Byron's "Cain"* joins Zillman's two editions of *Shelley's Prometheus Unbound* as an example of how the lack of a true theory of editing can vitiate years of industry and file drawers full of information.

I feel that the decision to include Steffan's edition of *Lord Byron's "Cain"* among the MLA Book Club selections was an especially unfortunate one. But because there is a lack of knowledge of editing procedures among editors of the Romantics themselves, it should not be surprising to find a similar dearth of knowledge and standards of judgment of editing in places of authority: among those who read and make editorial decisions for university presses and other scholarly publishers, among those who review such publications in learned journals, and among deans and department chairmen who provide tangible rewards for productive scholarship. In Elizabethan drama, the theoretical groundwork of bibliography laid by Pollard, Greg, and McKerrow was perhaps not as determinative in broadening the acceptance and implementation of improved textual standards as were the dedicated efforts of a handful of university teachers who sent out generations of students trained to understand, accept, inculcate, and enforce those higher standards. In the United States, those teachers have included Hyder Rollins and William A. Jackson at Harvard, and Fredson Bowers at Virginia. Among their students have been many of the leading exponents of textual analysis in other literary periods. In eighteenth-century studies a similar influence has been

exercised by Allen Hazen at Columbia and William Todd at
Texas. Many of the scholars of the Romantic period that I
know who have developed a serious interest and sound
knowledge of textual analysis are students of men deriving
from these traditions.

One of the greatest problems with developing a tradition
of sound textual scholarship in the Romantic period is that
so few of the senior scholars in the field have the interest
to guide their students to sound examples and authorities,
much less to enforce high standards among their colleagues. A substantive reason for this lack of enthusiasm
for collating texts it that the Romantic poets are still
ideologically alive. Their critics refuse to treat their works
as mere artifacts, but respond fully to their thought as well
as their artistry. Many of the finest scholars in the field are
deeply engaged in writing close-reading explications of
particular poems or surveys of epistemological, political, or
moral patterns in the literature of the period. They tend to
nod and mumble gratefully if someone, at no cost to them
in time or effort, provides a text printed with legible type
and wide margins suitable for extra-annotating. The
teacher-scholars who appreciate the vitality and genius of
the Romantics should recognize, however, that over the
past fifty years, hundreds or even thousands of students
have been driven away from the Romantics because of
false impressions about them generated in part by faulty
editing of their poetry. (Here I am speaking principally of
Shelley's text, though the editorial annotation of all
Romantic poetry has left room for considerable improvement down to the present day.) Because the Romantics
use approximately the same vocabulary we do, editors
have not felt it necessary to study the poets' usage and to
gloss special or unusual meanings of words. Thus critics
have mistaken Shelley's use of "Celtic," which he and his
contemporaries used in the Greek manner to designate
barbarians from the north that threatened the classical
Mediterranean civilization and cultural heritage. Critics
have likewise constantly misread various writers' use of

mother-in-law, sister-in-law, when they mean step-mother or step-sister. But far more fundamental to an edition than precise annotation is an accurate text. It is time, I believe, for critics to recognize that they have said about most poems all that can be usefully said before textual analysis establishes exactly what the poets wrote.

With this thought, let us return to the main subject with a consideration of the editorial situation as it regards Shelley's poetry. What has been happening in the recent past and what appears to lie ahead? The reappearance in 1948 of Shelley's rough draft notebooks, so long unavailable to scholars, has led to improved texts of a number of poems for which the sole authority is a holograph draft. "The Triumph of Life," "Charles the First," and a number of Shelley's posthumously published lyrics and translations have been brought nearer to Shelley's intention, though in several cases the unfinished state of the extant MSS will always leave scope for disagreement over details. Since 1964 Shelley's previously unpublished early shorter poems of the Esdaile Notebook have been published in full three times, making their substantive texts readily available. But all editing of this type, depending on a single authoritative manuscript, is child's play compared with reconstructing the author's text from a printed version through bibliographical analysis, and against this larger challenge, editors of Shelley's poetry have yet to prove themselves.

Shelley studies face, in fact, problems quite beyond those afflicting editing of the Romantic poets in general. I have already mentioned Lawrence John Zillman's two editions of *Prometheus Unbound*. The failures of his editorial principles are epitomized in a sentence in which he states that the editor must work to eliminate "the mannerisms to which the poet was subject."[6] Neville Rogers, editor of the forthcoming Clarendon Press edition of Shelley's poetry, has made pronouncements on editorial policy which have said, in effect, that the particular words

6. *Shelley's "Prometheus Unbound": The Text and the Drafts*, New Haven, Yale University Press, 1968, p. 25.

and punctuation Shelley employed are relatively unimportant because — to quote him — "the words on his page are no more than drops in the cascade of ideas which poured from that furiously rapid mind" and "despite his almost miraculous power of holding long, subtle and wonderful passages of Platonic syntax in his head, Shelley had neither the temperament nor the technique to make them intelligible to his readers by punctuation."[7] Professor Rogers' most recent editorial effort — a selection of Shelley's poetry published in the United States as Houghton Mifflin's Riverside Edition and in Great Britain by the Oxford University Press[8] — does not augur well for his projected edition. It contains errors of every imaginable sort. Shelley's poems are misnamed: "Lines written among the Euganean Hills," a poem in tetrameter couplets, becomes "Stanzas Written in the Euganean Hills" (p. viii), and "Ode to Liberty" becomes "Ode of Liberty" (p. 457). Biographical dates are confused, from the birthdates of William Shelley (p. xxi) and Queen Victoria (p. 471) to the death-dates of Fanny Imlay and Harriet Shelley (p. xxi). The publication date of Shelley's *Posthumous Poems* (p. 467) is given incorrectly, as is the year of the revolution in Naples to which Shelley alludes frequently in his letters and about which he wrote an important poem. Rogers confuses names of people: Rousseau's Saint-Preux becomes "Des Prieux" (p. xx and p. 463), Eliza O'Neill becomes Eliza "Neill." He gives Pisa rather than Venice as the setting of *Julian and Maddalo* (p. xxii). He truncates *Studia Neophilologica* to *Studia Philologica* (p. 462).

But two other limitations exhibit themselves in Rogers' recent publications that are far more significant so far as Rogers' qualifications as a textual editor are concerned.

7. Neville Rogers, "Shelley's Spelling: Theory and Practice," *Keats-Shelley Memorial Bulletin* 16, 1965, p. 21; and "The Punctuation of Shelley's Syntax," *Keats-Shelley Memorial Bulletin* 17, 1966, p. 23.

8. Percy Bysshe Shelley, *Selected Poetry* (Riverside Edition), ed. Neville Rogers, Boston, Houghton Mifflin, 1968; Percy Bysshe Shelley, *Selected Poetry*, ed. Neville Rogers, London, Oxford, New York, Oxford University Press, 1969.

The first, paralleling his imaginative rearrangement of facts, is his imaginative reordering of words he is supposedly quoting. Second is his tendency to rationalize his limitations into critical principles. If *he* does not quote accurately, the precise words are of little concern; if *he* ignores the principles of bibliographical analysis or textual criticism, those who attempt to employ such methodologies have (and I quote) "for the devoted learning and accomplishment flowering around 1492 . . . substituted a merely professional cleverness and efficiency with small, mechanical (yclepèd 'scientific') skills."[9] And, even more disastrously, if *he* has not updated his text of one of Shelley's poems to conform with what he himself agrees is the text Shelley intended, he can write critical notes to justify the corrupted text he chooses to reprint. Let me cite one specific example: in the Riverside Shelley, Rogers begins his notes on "The Triumph of Life" by observing that (though he reprints the version edited by Thomas Hutchinson in 1904) "the text has been emended and expanded by subsequent editors." A few lines below this admission appears this note: "The blank spaces in lines 115 and 175 are examples of Shelley's unwillingness to slow down his rapid composition when he could not, momentarily, hit on the right word or syllables: his MSS frequently contain these blanks, which he intended to fill up later" (p. 460). Unfortunately for Rogers' generalization, one of the lines he cites does *not* contain blanks in Shelley's manuscript but reads (as Geoffrey Matthews' text and mine firmly agree): "And frost in these performs what fire in those." In the other instance, I at least am convinced that Shelley intended the passage to read: "When Freedom left those who upon the Free / Had bound a yoke" (115-116), leaving no blanks whatsoever in the two lines cited.[10]

9. Neville Rogers, "Shelley: Texts and Pretexts, The Case of First Editions," *Keats-Shelley Memorial Bulletin* 19, 1968, p. 46.
10. See G. M. Matthews, "'The Triumph of Life': A New Text," *Studia Neophilologica* 32, 1960, pp. 271-329; and Donald H. Reiman, *Shelley's "The*

Progress in editing Shelley is, however, being made and
will be made. G. M. Matthews is working on the Longmans
Shelley which, whatever limitations the series imposes with
regard to the critical apparatus, will undoubtedly have a
text much better than any collected edition of Shelley's
poetry currently available. Judith Chernaik, in a critical
study of Shelley's lyrics forthcoming from the Press of
Case Western Reserve University, has re-edited most of
Shelley's best lyrics from the manuscripts and early
printings. Timothy Webb of the University of Leeds has
published a new text of Shelley's translation of Homer's
"Hymn to Venus" and is working on an edition of all
Shelley's translations from Greek and Latin. R. B.
Woodings hopes to publish soon his text of "Charles the
First." Irving Massey, Stuart Curran, and Joseph Raben
have probed special textual problems in Shelley.

None of the above-named scholars, or anyone else that I
am aware of now working in Shelley studies, has had the
benefit of first-rate training in modern textual criticism.
And there has been no solid attempt to apply the methods
of textual criticism to the editions published during
Shelley's lifetime. (It may have been partly the dearth of
such studies in the primary area of need that led Fredson
Bowers some years ago to hail as extremely important
Charles H. Taylor's slim but sound volume entitled *The
Early Collected Editions of Shelley's Poetry*,[11] which
analyzed the transmission of Shelley's text from the first
editions through the piracies of the 1820s and 1830s to
Mary Shelley's first collected edition of 1839.) In the
hope, however, that scholars trained in textual analysis will
soon begin to undertake systematic study of Shelley's
poetry, I should like to conclude this paper by suggesting
how such a study might begin and proceed.

First, the volume of Shelley's poems that would provide

Triumph of Life": *A Critical Study, Based on a Text Newly Edited from the
Bodleian Manuscript*, Urbana, University of Illinois Press, 1965.

11. The book is subtitled: *A Study in the History and Transmission of the
Printed Text*, New Haven, Yale University Press, 1958. Bowers' review
appeared in *Keats-Shelley Journal* 9, 1960, pp. 35-38.

the best opportunity for such analysis is *Hellas*. For *Hellas* the press-copy — Edward Williams' fair copy with Shelley's corrections — survives in the Huntington Library. *Hellas* was printed by Samuel and Richard Bentley, who had printed *Epipsychidion* a year earlier, and a study of their press style in printing *Hellas*, in conjunction with a study of other poetic texts printed by the Bentley brothers during the early 1820s for which press-copy may survive, might lead naturally into textual analysis of *Epipsychidion*. There are two rather simple ways to study the house style of C. H. Reynell, printer of *History of a Six Weeks' Tour* (1817), *Rosalind and Helen* (1819), the second edition of *The Cenci* (1821), and *Posthumous Poems* (1824): First one can analyze the changes made in *The Cenci* from the first edition, printed by Glauco Masi of Livorno under Shelley's supervision, to the second edition, which was printed by Reynell, using the first edition as copy text. Similarly, one can study changes made by Reynell when he reprinted *Alastor* in *Posthumous Poems*, using the first edition as copy text. Next, one can study some fragments of press-copy that survive for these and other volumes of poetry published by Reynell to determine what changes in orthography and punctuation would have originated in the printing house. Once Reynell's house-style has been examined, bibliographers could move on to that of Marchant, the printer of *Prometheus Unbound*. One helpful place to begin might be a comparative analysis of the two volumes of Ollier's edition of *The Works of Charles Lamb* (1818), the second volume printed by Reynell and the first by Marchant.

There are available to would-be textual critics of the period at least five general printers' manuals published between 1808 and 1841[12] there is a book on the patents

12. Caleb Stower, *The Printer's Grammar*, London, 1808; John Johnson, *Typographia, or The Printer's Instructor*, London, 1824; Thomas C. Hansard, *Typographia*, London, 1825; Charles H. Timperley, *The Printer's Manual*, London, 1838; William Savage, *A Dictionary of the Art of Printing*, London, 1841. These titles have recently been reprinted as Volumes 4-8 in Series 3: Printers' Manuals, of *English Bibliographical Sources*, ed. David F. Foxon.

taken out for various improvements in printing presses
from 1617 to 1866, which outlines the technical developments available to the printer;[13] there are Ellic Howe's
account(s) of *The London Compositor*[14] and Shorter's
study of English paper mills.[15] The basic techniques of
textual analysis have been worked out, challenged, and
polished by bibliographers and textual critics working with
incunabula, with books of the English Renaissance and
eighteenth century, and — most recently — with major
American authors of the nineteenth century. All that is
needed is that someone committed to overcoming the
problems connected with Shelley's text direct his efforts
to analysis of the transmission of those texts of Shelley's
poetry, taking the initiative away from those who cannot
distinguish an accidental from a substantive feature, who
do not understand the criteria for selecting and emending a
copy text, and who persist in thinking it the duty of an
editor to alter features of the best authorities on the basis
of their own whimsical preferences.

It ought to be possible to create within a few years, a
climate in which the influence of incompetent editors
would be curtailed in Romantic studies as effectively as it
has been among Shakespeareans. One of the surest ways in
which the standards of scholarly editing could be improved
would be for foundations, publishers, and librarians with
significant manuscript collections to withhold their support from individuals whose only claim to edit the writings
of a major figure is priority in the field. If someone has
had the diligence to collect numerous photostats and make
approximate transcriptions of them, but has exhibited
neither editorial acumen nor enough intellectual curiosity

13. *Printing Patents: Abridgments of Patent Specifications Relating to
Printing, 1617-1857 (with Supplement, 1858-1866)*, with introduction by
James Harrison, London, Printing Historical Society, 1969.
14. Ellic Howe, ed., *The London Compositor: Documents relating to
Wages, Working Conditions and Customs of the London Printing Trade,
1785-1900*, London, The Bibliographical Society, 1947.
15. Alfred H. Shorter, *Paper Mills and Paper Makers in England, 1495-1800*,
Hilversum, Holland, The Paper Publications Society, 1957.

to master the techniques and to acquire the knowledge necessary for superior editing, he should be encouraged by every positive and negative persuasion either to learn his trade or to collaborate with a scholar who has demonstrated that mastery. And if a scholarly press cannot tell whether or not a manuscript exhibits such standards until the edition is reviewed, it ought seriously to re-examine its publishing policies or its editorial personnel.

But the climate about which I am speaking that will stimulate and support editorial excellence will not initially be generated by foundation executives, publishers, or curators of rare book and manuscript collections. It must begin among textual scholars in all periods of English literature and among scholars of the Romantic period — those who direct dissertations or serve on dissertation committees, those who review newly-published editions, and those who lecture to their students and colleagues on editing the Romantics. It must begin at conferences like this and spread throughout all levels of the profession on both sides of the Atlantic. Speaking with a group of scholars who *are* interested in improving standards of editing in the period, I can articulate candidly those truths that are difficult to direct to those who need them most. Had I more — to use a fashionable word — *chutzpah*, I would say *directly* to the man who lacks the wit or who refuses to undergo the discipline necessary to edit with accuracy, knowledge, and understanding: "You may teach the unlettered; you may golf, fish, garden, and retail academic gossip. I will drink with you at MLA and invite you to my home for dinner; if you have certain other important humane virtues, I'll even approve of your marrying my daughter. But one thing I ask: Please keep your hands off my literary heritage."

Annotating Wordsworth

W. J. B. Owen

Most papers offered to this Conference, to my recollection, have been concerned with the editorial process
(either in abstract theory or with practical reference to
particular authors and works) of establishing the correct
text — meaning the text the author wished, or may be
presumed to have wished, to present to his public. I have
been engaged for a good many years now in this process as
it applies to William Wordsworth, somewhat in his verse
but mainly in his prose;[1] and, with rare exceptions, I have

1. This paper emerges mainly from my experience in editing, with
Professor Jane Worthington Smyser, Wordsworth's *Prose Works* for the
Clarendon Press, and from sketches for a Commentary on *The Prelude*.
Excerpts from the prose are cited by volume and page of the Oxford edition
(*Prose*), which is in page-proof as I write; *The Prelude* is cited, usually in the
text of 1805, from the edition of Ernest de Selincourt, revised by Helen
Darbishire (Oxford, 1959) (*Prel.*). Wordsworth's letters are quoted from the
edition of Ernest de Selincourt (Oxford, 1935-39), and where possible from
the revised volumes by Chester L. Shaver, Mary Moorman, and Alan G. Hill
(Oxford, 1967-70), cited as *E.Y.*, *M.Y.*, and *L.Y.* I have drawn some examples
from *The Prelude*, and some sentences of comment on them, from my paper
"Literary Echoes in *The Prelude*," read at the second Wordsworth Summer
School at Rydal Mount, July 1971, and published in *The Wordsworth Circle*,
3, No. 1 (Winter 1972), pp. 3-16, and used here with the permission of the
editor.

found that the editing of Wordsworth in this sense is not very difficult intellectually. It has often been laborious, in that some works (such as the prose documents connected with *Lyrical Ballads*) were revised by Wordsworth in edition after edition, and complex collations are therefore required. It has often been laborious also, in the case of works, published or unpublished, which exist in manuscript, in that the hand of the poet himself, and the hands of some of his amanuenses when they are writing rapidly, are abominably difficult; and reading manuscripts is often made harder by the poet's habit of revising, time and again, in interlinear spaces which are too small for his revisions. These are difficulties, however, which can usually be overcome by dogged returns to the manuscript and determination not to give up until the printer sends his final proof. And when these difficulties are overcome — if they can be overcome — the editor is rarely in doubt what he should print. In the range of Wordsworth's prose I recall perhaps two problems in the philosophy of editing which exercised us: the easier one was concerned with the unnamed piece contributed to *The Friend* in 1809-10 which I call *Reply to Mathetes*, where it rapidly became clear that, wherever possible, we should follow the manuscript in the Forster Collection[2] rather than the printed text of 1809-10 and, *a fortiori*, rather than later printings of *The Friend* — for while the manuscript has Wordsworthian authority, the printed text, as far as we can discover, has not. The larger problem is concerned with manuscripts connected with the *Guide to the Lakes* in its various forms. We (I should say mainly Professor Smyser) distinguished two kinds of manuscript among the many which survive at Grasmere: one kind concerned with drafts for the printed book, either in its earliest form as an

2. See *The Friend*, ed. Barbara E. Rooke, London and Princeton, 1969, I, pp. lxxxvi-lxxxviii, II, pp. 379-87. Miss Rooke's general plan, to use *The Friend* of 1818 as copy-text and to reprint the serial publication of 1809-10 as an Appendix, is, I believe, correct for the Collected Coleridge, though (as I indicate below and have said at greater length elsewhere) I believe that she should have taken greater cognizance of the manuscript.

Introduction to Joseph Wilkinson's series of plates called
*Select Views in Cumberland, Westmoreland, and Lanca-
shire* (1810), or with the book as it is more generally
known – and here there was no problem: we simply put
the manuscript readings, with the variants of printed texts,
in the apparatus. The other kind of manuscript, we came
to realise, though it talked about the same things as the
Guide to the Lakes, talked about them so differently, and
in a so much more detailed way than does the *Guide*, that
we separated them out, and will print them separately as a
hitherto unpublished work which we have called the
Unpublished Tour.

But for the rest we have usually proceeded on conven-
tional lines, following Wordsworth's own injunction (I
believe frowned upon in some quarters) to print, in the
case of published works, the author's final text: "you
know," he wrote to Alexander Dyce in April 1830, "what
importance I attach to following strictly the last copy of
the text of an Author" (*L.Y.*, p. 473). Occasionally we
have not done this, especially when Wordsworth wrote
nonsense or revised his own text so as to make nonsense
of it. For instance, in the *Guide to the Lakes* Wordsworth
printed, in the three separate editions of the book (1822,
1823, 1835) the astonishing observation that "this country
[= area, district] is bounded on the south and east by the
sea" (*Prose*, II, p. 187); if it was in Wordsworth's time, the
layout of Britain must have changed remarkably in the last
hundred and fifty years, so we emend to "this country is
bounded on the south and west by the sea" (yet all
editors, I believe, including Ernest de Selincourt in his
edition of 1906, reprinted 1970, the best which has yet
appeared, reprint "east"). In the Preface to Wordsworth's
Poems of 1815, near the end, he summarizes and quotes,
as an instance of the workings of the faculty he calls
Fancy, Charles Cotton's Ode called *Winter*. His summary
reads thus, in the text of 1849-50, Wordsworth's last
published edition:

The middle part of this ode contains a most lively

description of the entrance of Winter, with his retinue, as 'A palsied king,' and yet a military monarch, — advancing for conquest with his army; the several bodies of which, and their arms and equipments, are described with a rapidity of detail, and a profusion of *fanciful* comparisons, which indicate on the part of the poet extreme activity of intellect, and a correspondent hurry of delightful feeling. Winter retires from the foe into his fortress, where

> — 'a magazine
> Of sovereign juice is cellared in;
> Liquor that will the siege maintain
> Should Phœbus ne'er return again.'

(*Prose*, III, pp. 37-38)

If you did not wince when I read "Winter retires from the foe into his fortress," you are one with a numerous company of Wordsworthian editors and readers who pass by such errors without thinking. For it is clear, if you read Cotton's poem, and probably even if you do not, that it is not Winter who retires into a fortress, but the poet, besieged by "the foe," Winter, and fortifying himself with "sovereign juice." And so Wordsworth's early texts of this Preface (1815, 1820) show; for they read, and the Oxford text will read, not "Winter retires," but "He retires." In the edition of 1827, for some reason known only to himself (or perhaps not known), Wordsworth (presumably) altered the reading to "Winter"; and editors, apart from myself and from the few who reprint Wordsworth's earliest rather than his latest text, have followed blindly the text of 1849-50. They have thereby revealed that they prefer to *reprint* Wordsworth rather than to understand him and then make him understandable to those who read modern editions.

I am thus led to the first, perhaps the only, point of editorial philosophizing which I wish to make and which will help to explain the title I chose to put at the head of this paper. It is this: that every editor of a text ought also to be a commentator on the text, whether or not he actually writes down a commentary. I mean that every editor ought to be certain, or as certain as he can be, of the meaning of every word and phrase and sentence in his text, and should be prepared to defend his text, if challenged, with a convincing explanation of it or commentary on it. Wordsworth is himself a guide who deserves respectful treatment: writing to Walter Scott on 7 November 1805, about Scott's edition of Dryden, he generalizes thus:

> A correct text is the first object of an editor: then such notes as explain difficult or unintelligible passages or throw light upon them; and lastly, which is of much less importance, notes pointing out passages or authors to which the Poet has been indebted, not in the piddling way of [a] phrase here and phrase there (which is detestable as a general practice) but where the Poet has really had essential obligations either as to matter or to manner. (*E.Y.*, p. 642)

My immediate point is that a "correct text" of Wordsworth does not necessarily emerge by mechanical reproduction of the author's latest text, and that, when it does not so emerge, the editor is stepping, whether formally or not, into Wordsworth's second field of editorial activity, the production of "such notes as explain difficult or unintelligible passages or throw light upon them."

Difficulty or unintelligibility is not always recognized by the editor; or, rather, the one is mistaken for the other: the passage that is merely difficult is thought to be unintelligible, and the editor takes steps to remedy the unintelligibility. Let me quote four passages from Wordsworth's prose, three from published works and one from an unpublished essay. In his pamphlet on *The Convention of Cintra* (1809) Wordsworth writes:

> . . . how inefficient for all good purposes are the tools and implements of policy, compared with these mighty engines of Nature! — There is no middle course: two masters cannot be served: — Justice must either be enthroned above might, and the moral law take place of the edicts of selfish passion; or the heart of the people, which alone can sustain the efforts of the people, will languish. . . . (*Prose*, I, p. 292)

In the *Reply to Mathetes* which Wordsworth contributed to *The Friend*, he writes about

> works of pure science, or of the combined faculties of imagination, feeling, and reason; — works which, both from their independence in their origin upon accident, their nature,

> their duration, and the wide spread of their influence, are
> entitled rightly to take place of the noblest and most
> beneficent deeds of Heroes, Statesmen, Legislators, or War-
> riors. (*Prose*, II, p. 19)

In an unpublished essay on the *Sublime and Beautiful*,
connected with the *Guide to the Lakes*, he writes about
the effect of what he calls "Power" as an element in the
Sublime:

> But if that Power which is exalted above our sympathy
> impresses the mind with personal fear, so as the sensation
> becomes more lively than the impression or thought of the
> exciting cause, then self-consideration & all its accompanying
> littleness takes place of the sublime, & wholly excludes it.
> (*Prose*, II, p. 354)

In the *Guide to the Lakes* itself, Wordsworth, objecting to
the white-washing of houses, comments:

> The mere aspect of cleanliness and neatness thus given, not
> only to an individual house, but, where the practice is general,
> to the whole face of the country, produces moral associations
> so powerful, that, in many minds, they take place of all others.
> (*Prose*, II, pp. 215-16)

You will perceive that I am establishing the Wordsworthian
idiom "take place of." The meaning of this phrase, which
is by no means confined to Wordsworthian usage, is
perfectly well recognized in *O.E.D.*, s.v. *place*, sb., sense
27.c: "take precedence of." But at least one editor of *The
Convention of Cintra* reads, without notice, "take the
place of"; a recent editor of *The Friend* emends the phrase
to "take [the] place of" with due notice of editorial
brackets; as no one has yet printed the essay on the
Sublime and Beautiful in full, we shall take the opportunity of printing the Wordsworthian reading in the Oxford
edition as Wordsworth wrote it — even though the
Clarendon Press proof-reader queried the reading "take
place" in our text of the *Guide to the Lakes* which
supplies my fourth example. The editors who emended the
phrase in *The Convention of Cintra* and *The Friend*, and
the Press proof-reader, thought that what was merely, for
late nineteenth-century and twentieth-century readers, a

difficult (in fact unfamiliar and obsolete) idiom was unintelligible, and took steps, or proposed steps, to make it intelligible. In fact they make it unintelligible: how could one possibly say with logic that "works of pure science" "are entitled to take [the] place of the noblest and most beneficent deeds of Heroes, Statesmen, Legislators, or Warriors"? Or in my third example, what would be the sense of saying that something "takes [the] place of the sublime, & wholly excludes it"? If A takes the place of B, it necessarily excludes it, and there is no need to say so; if A takes place of B, it does not necessarily exclude it. The "moral associations" that go with whiteness may be the major associations connected with white houses, but obviously they are not the only associations, as they would be if they were to "take [the] place of all other" associations.

Here is another instance of editorial tampering, from Wordsworth's correspondence: on 29 March 1809 Wordsworth wrote to De Quincey on the subject of the dispatches of Sir John Moore and other relevant documents on the Peninsular War which had recently been laid on the table of the House of Commons. Wordsworth was concerned about the accuracy of these dispatches and especially about the anti-Spanish feeling which they might generate in Britain; and in this letter he gives De Quincey hints for the Postscript which De Quincey eventually added to Wordsworth's pamphlet on *The Convention of Cintra*. Among Wordsworth's complaints is that (according to the editors, de Selincourt and, latterly, Mary Moorman) "the fate of Castanos is totally misrepresented – inasmuch as his centre only was defeated, his two wings being untouched, part of which retired south and part threw themselves into Saragossa, where they made, as we know, a most valiant resistance" (*M.Y.*, I, p. 307). I look at the foot of de Selincourt's or Mrs. Moorman's page, and I find a footnote to "fate" in the phrase "the fate of Castanos is totally misrepresented": "*Written* fact." The editors appear to have no doubt of their emendation: Wordsworth

wrote "fact" when he meant "fate." I suggest that when
he wrote "fact" he meant "fact," and that by "the fact of
Castanos" he meant "the facts about / the truth about
Castanos"; because that is, indeed, what he is writing
about – the accuracy or inaccuracy of Moore's account of
facts, not a sentimental reaction to the personal fate of a
Spanish general.

In all or most of these cases, the old principle of
difficilior lectio praestat might have guided the editors; the
trouble was that, in each case, *difficilior*, which was also
recta lectio, seemed to the editor *nulla lectio*. There are, in
my view, occasional passages in Wordsworth where *nulla
lectio* must remain, where the text is unintelligible and
where the unintelligibility should be allowed to stand,
covered, of course, by a note from the editor. In all early
manuscripts of *The Prelude*, Book II, which contain the
passage, I believe, lines 19-21 (of the text of 1805) read
thus:

> Ah! is there one who ever has been young,
> And needs a monitory voice to tame
> The pride of virtue, and of intellect?

This reading survives into MS D, and is there revised to:

> Ah! is there one who ever has been young,
> Nor needs a warning voice to tame the pride
> Of intellect and virtue's self-esteem?

The point at issue is: "And" versus "Nor" at the beginning
of line 20. It is clear that Wordsworth thinks he is writing a
rhetorical question of the form: "Is there anyone who is A
and who is not B?" which implies: "Everyone who is A is
also B." "Is there anyone who is deeply interested in
Wordsworth and who has not read *The Prelude* often?" is
such a question; it implies: "Everyone who is interested in
Wordsworth has read *The Prelude* often." In fact Wordsworth's question is exactly opposite in form to this, and he
did not correct his error until he came to revise MS D. In
my view, an editor who sets out (as several do, and with
justification) to reproduce MS A of the poem should retain
the error in his text and draw attention to it in his notes. I

had hoped that I would be the first editor or annotator of *The Prelude* to do this; but, unfortunately for me, and fortunately for students of the poem, the point has recently been made in J. C. Maxwell's parallel-text edition, published in 1971 by Penguin Books.

Let me repeat the proposition that an editor of Wordsworth is also an annotator of Wordsworth, implicitly or explicitly, whether or not a formal commentary is part of his edition. The implicit commentary assures the editor that he has understood his author, and that where his author is unintelligible, and where for one reason or another it is desirable that the unintelligible text should stand, the implicit commentary assures the editor that he is aware of what he is doing when he prints an unintelligible text. The bare bones of an explicit commentary, in my view, should do the same for the reader: assuring *him* that the editor has considered every passage the meaning of which might be difficult, or (what is often worse) ambiguous or misleading, for readers of the editor's generation.

Within this proposition, and in several related observations I have made, lies the justification for the commentary in the sense of an explanation of words and phrases which are to the modern reader difficult, ambiguous, or misleading, occurring in passages where the text is not in doubt and is in no need of establishment. I think (to take a simple instance) of passages such as this from the *Reply to Mathetes*:

> These expectations are not immoderate: they demand nothing more than the perception of a few plain truths; namely that Knowledge efficacious for the production of virtue, is the ultimate end of all effort, the sole dispenser of complacency and repose. (*Prose*, II, p. 19)

Or this, from the *Guide to the Lakes* (it is from the discussion of the effect of white buildings on landscape from which I took an earlier example):

> The continental traveller also will remember, that the convents hanging from the rocks of the Rhine, the Rhone, the Danube, or among the Appenines, or the mountains of Spain,

are not looked at with less complacency when, as is often the case, they happen to be of a brilliant white. (*Prose*, II, p. 216)

Or this, from Book XI of *The Prelude* (29-31), where Wordsworth, talking about (as the title of the book puts it) "Imagination, How Impaired and Restored," welcomes the Spring, and Nature in Spring, as a "counterpoise" to "the spirit of evil":

> So neither were complacency nor peace
> Nor tender yearnings wanting for my good
> Through those distracted times.

Or this, from *The Recluse* (301-6), where Wordsworth utters a "hail" to Grasmere

> And to whatever else of outward form
> Can give us inward help, can purify,
> And elevate, and harmonise, and soothe,
> And steal away, and for a while deceive
> And lap in pleasing rest, and bear us on
> Without desire in full complacency ...

Someone (but I do not know that anyone has) ought to have pointed out that Wordsworth's use of *complacency* is unusual by twentieth-century standards: it means, in the *O.E.D.* definition (s.v., sense 1), "tranquil ... satisfaction," not, as in the *O.E.D.* definition of what seems to be twentieth-century usage, "self-satisfaction" (s.v., sense 2).

This kind of commentary depends upon linguistic information readily available to the scholar and (I am sorry to say) too infrequently used; its existence depends upon an alertness of mind — of the sort that is easily stimulated to say: "That's an odd expression" or "What does that mean?" — which (I am sorry to say) not all editors of Wordsworth seem to have had or at least to have exercised consistently.

Another kind of commentary depends for its effective-ness, not on mere linguistic information, but on factual knowledge. The proof-reader assigned by the Clarendon Press to Wordsworth's *Prose Works* often displayed that alertness of mind to which I have just referred as an

editorial virtue, though he did not think it his duty to
answer the questions he proposed. He was suspicious of a
phrase which occurs in the *Guide to the Lakes* in a passage
in which Wordsworth gives directions to the tourist:

> crossing the Lake [Windermere] by the Ferry — then pass the
> two villages of Sawrey, and on quitting the latter, you have a
> fine view of the Lake of Esthwaite. (*Prose*, II p. 162)

He questioned the phrase "the two villages of Sawrey,"
but I imagine that, if he had been familiar with the Lake
District to the extent of knowing that, as you leave the
west side of the Windermere ferry by the obvious road,
you pass first through the village of Far Sawrey and then
through the village of Near Sawrey, he would not have had
his alertness tickled to the extent of questioning "the two
villages of Sawrey" as an odd-sounding phrase that might
be wrong.

Another kind of difficulty can be solved by the
application of information less generally available, either
inside or outside the experience of the well-read Wordsworthian. Forgive me if I refer briefly to two passages in
The Prelude on which I have already published my
findings. In Book VII Wordsworth describes the oppressive
effect of the mere multeity of the passing crowds in
London streets:

> Thus have I look'd, nor ceas'd to look, oppress'd
> By thoughts of what, and whither, when and how,
> Until the shapes before my eyes became
> A second-sight procession, such as glides
> Over still mountains, or appears in dreams.
>   (VII.598-602)

The editorial jar, stirring, or tickle should, in my view,
begin with the identification of London crowds with "A
second-sight procession, such as glides/ Over still mountains." "Procession" is easy, but why "second-sight," and
why, especially, "glides/ Over still mountains"? Because,
apparently, of a Lake District legend which alleged that
either a single spectral horseman furiously galloping or a
procession of dignified mounted warriors had from time to

time been seen on Southerfell and reported by local inhabitants. So Wordsworth used the legend, anyway, in *An Evening Walk* (text of 1793, lines 179-90, and Wordsworth's note), where he says that he got the story from James Clarke's *Survey of the Lakes of Cumberland, Westmorland, and Lancashire* (London, 1787, 1789). And there is a curious passage in a manuscript draft for *The Prelude* (*Prel.*, p. 533) which indicates that Wordsworth himself, when he was a mere schoolboy, saw the military procession (perhaps because he had heard the legend or read of it elsewhere) in a visionary or dream-experience — hence, I would suppose, the odd qualification "*second-sight* procession" and the phrase "appears in dreams." No editor that I know of has bothered to explain this curious image: I can only assume that no one found it difficult, or, if anyone did, that he concealed his ignorance in silence.

At least one commentator, the late Raymond Dexter Havens, the second part of whose massive *The Mind of a Poet*[3] represents a first step towards the kind of commentary on *The Prelude* which I envisage as a possibility, confessed his inability to explicate my next passage, which occurs in its fullest form in various intermediate versions of *The Prelude*, Book IV. If man, says Wordsworth in MS A, lacks what he calls "religious dignity of mind," he "Seems but a pageant plaything with vile claws." He seems something more specific in later developments of this image:

> Seems but a piece of fearful mechanism
> Vile as the Tyger's which the barbarous East
> Constructs, to lodge within her palace walls (A^2C)
>
> Seems but a piece of fearful mechanism
> An oriental plaything with vile claws (B^2)
>
> Is but a piece of fearful mechanism
> Vile as the Tygers, which, with skill perverse
> And monstrous, Tyrants of the barbarous East
> Construct to growl within their palace walls (D)
>
> (IV.297-302 and app. crit.)

3. Baltimore, 1941. See p. 364.

"Is the reference to some sort of cage or to a mechanism peculiar to eastern palaces?" asked Havens. I do not know how he arrived at the notion of a cage, but his second alternative was obviously on the right lines. There is such a "mechanism peculiar to eastern palaces" which fits all the details of Wordsworth's various descriptions: it is a tiger, it was constructed by (or at least to the order of) a tyrant of the barbarous East, it has vile claws, and it growls when you turn the crank-handle near the tiger's left shoulder and thereby operate a small organ inside the body. It is the object called "Tipu's Tiger" which is now in the Victoria and Albert Museum; it was built to the order of the East India Company's thorn in the flesh, Tipu Sultan, captured at the fall of Seringapatam in 1799, and held by the East India Company in London from 1800 till about 1850 — indeed it was on display in Leadenhall Street from 1808. Wordsworth, who had direct connections with the Company through his brother John and only less direct through Charles Lamb, must have known about the tiger, which in any case was famous in the first half of the nineteenth century and constantly referred to in books on Indian affairs.[4]

I have virtually moved from the province of verbal explication to the province of source-material in a commentary: in these last two instances, verbal explication is in effect served by, or dependent upon, a knowledge of source-material, whether by that one means a literary source or a physical or even metaphysical object obscurely referred to by the author. Other ends may be served as one tries to meet Wordsworth's own requirement: "notes pointing out passages or authors to which the Poet has been indebted." It is, I believe, of interest to know merely that in such and such a passage the author is, or is not, original; that, if he is not original, he follows his source or differs from it; that, if he differs from it, he does so by design or by carelessness or by misunderstanding — and at

4. For more detailed discussion of these passages see *N. & Q.* 214, 1969, pp. 49-50, and 215, 1970, pp. 379-80.

that point I will pause, deferring till later a possible further step in the commentator's activity.

For an instance where Wordsworth is not original, consider his description of the scene from the top of Snowdon in the last book of *The Prelude*:

> I looked about, and lo!
> The Moon stood naked in the Heavens, at height
> Immense above my head, and on the shore
> I found myself of a huge sea of mist,
> Which, meek and silent, rested at my feet:
> A hundred hills their dusky backs upheaved
> All over this still Ocean . . .
>
> (XIII.40-46)

A recent book on Wordsworth's aesthetics which does not recognize the unoriginality of the last line and a half comments enthusiastically: "Here the surrounding hills are mantled with mist — so that the poet sees and feels their animal life at the very moment that he apprehends them . . . In these lines, the imaginative attribution of animal movement to hills can be traced to a genuine act of perception, a moment of real human feeling."[5] Perhaps the poet did "see and feel [the] animal life" of the hills, but if so his "genuine act of perception" issued in a strikingly unoriginal way. For the phrase which excites this critic is not Wordsworth's, but Milton's, in his description of God's separation of the land from the water in *Paradise Lost*, Book VII:

> God said
> Be gather'd now ye Waters under Heav'n
> Into one place, and let dry land appeer.
> Immediately the Mountains huge appeer
> Emergent, and thir broad bare backs upheave
> Into the Clouds, thir tops ascend the Skie:
> So high as heav'd the tumid Hills, so low
> Down sunk a hollow bottom broad and deep,
> Capacious bed of Waters.
>
> (VII.282-90)

5. J. A. W. Heffernan, *Wordsworth's Theory of Poetry*, Ithaca, 1969, p. 36.

My own reaction to Wordsworth's description is also enthusiastic, but not for the reason given by Mr. Heffernan. I shall define it more precisely later.

Here is what one might call the opposite case, where Wordsworth's borrowing is acknowledged and obvious, but where my reaction is far from enthusiastic. In the second *Essay upon Epitaphs*, Wordsworth quotes with disapproval an epitaph on Philip Sidney which, says his source (John Weever's *Ancient Funeral Monuments*, 1631), and as Wordsworth also records, is a mere adaptation from a French epitaph (by du Bellay) on a French General. He places this poem in juxtaposition with a prose passage from Weever on which he comments:

> Yet Weever, in a foregoing Paragraph thus expresses himself upon the same Subject; giving without his knowledge, in my opinion, an example of the manner in which such an Epitaph ought to have been composed. — "But here I cannot pass over in silence Sir Philip Sidney the elder brother, being (to use Camden's words) the glorious star of this family, a lively pattern of virtue, and the lovely joy of all the learned sort . . .

— and so forth for ten more lines of prose. Wordsworth comments:

> There can be no need to analyse this simple effusion of the moment in order to contrast it with the laboured composition before given: the difference will flash upon the Reader at once. (*Prose*, II, p. 72)

Now it is quite possible that the reader will react in this way; but, uncomfortably for Wordsworth's argument, the passage which he admires is not a "simple effusion of the moment," and, in giving this account of Sidney, Weever is not "expressing himself." He is, as his own parenthesis indicates, quoting Camden, not only in the phrases surrounding the parenthesis which I quoted, but in the whole prose tribute to Sidney; and indeed not Camden, who wrote the passage in Latin in his *Britannia*, but rather Philemon Holland, who translated the Latin into the English which Weever and Wordsworth quote. And the Latin, when you look at it, is far from being a "simple effusion of the moment": it is elegant and well-meditated Renaissance Latin prose. Strained through Holland's English and misinterpreted as a spontaneous overflow of John Weever's powerful feelings at the recollection of Sidney's achievement and sacrifice, it is, through the eyes of the alert commentator, a splendid example of the unreliability of the canon of sincerity as a criterion of literary merit which Wordsworth is here canvassing.

I have assumed in what I have just been saying that sources can be firmly identified. This is often the case with Wordsworth, who did not scruple to steal from anybody handy, with or without acknowledgement. In the third *Essay upon Epitaphs*, for instance, he cites, at fairly wide intervals and with the air of one who has every vicious eighteenth-century epitaph at his command, epitaphs by William Mason on Mrs. Mason, by Mason again on a certain Miss Drummond, and by Thomas Gray on Mrs. Clarke (*Prose*, II, pp. 82, 85, 86-87). In fact he almost certainly found these three epitaphs printed, one after the other in the order in which he uses them, in the famous, or infamous, eighteenth-century anthology called *Elegant Extracts in Verse* — which he does indeed name in the Essay (*Prose*, II, p. 84), but not in connection with these epitaphs. I am not saying that this is dishonest, only that the commentator provides a truer picture of Wordsworth's methods of working than the uninformed reader might conjure up, or than Wordsworth might have wished him to conjure up.

Sometimes sources are less obvious, and in such instances I wish to enter a plea for caution on the part of the commentator. In the first book of *The Prelude*, Wordsworth lists various themes which (so he says) he had in mind as bases for an epic poem. One of them would have told

> how the Friends
> And Followers of Sertorius, out of Spain
> Flying, found shelter in the Fortunate Isles;
> And left their usages, their arts, and laws,
> To disappear by a slow gradual death;

To dwindle and to perish one by one
Starved in those narrow bounds; but not the Soul
Of Liberty, which fifteen hundred years
Surviv'd, and, when the European came
With skill and power that could not be withstood,
Did, like a pestilence, maintain its hold,
And wasted down by glorious death that Race
Of natural Heroes.

(I.189-201)

The Oxford edition of *The Prelude* quotes at great length from North's translation of Plutarch's Life of Sertorius, which tells the story of Sertorius's voyage, but not, of course, of the subjugation of his colony by the Spaniards. The Oxford commentary also alleges that Wordsworth read Plutarch "in the French translation of Thevet (1676) of which a copy was in his library"; and for the later history of the descendants of Sertorius it refers to "Alonso de Espinosa . . . *The Guanches of Teneriffe*, first published in Spanish in 1594" (*Prel.*, pp. 514-15).

Here is a splendid train of misinformation which arises from the incaution of de Selincourt and Miss Darbishire and which is repeated in every edition of the poem known to me which revises, adapts, or steals from the Oxford edition. It is very plain that Wordsworth knew Plutarch, but there is (I believe) no French translation by Thevet dated 1676, even though the catalogue of the sale of Wordsworth's library suggests that there is. There is an edition of North's English translation of that date which contains "The lives of twenty selected eminent persons . . . translated out of the work of that famous historiographer to the King of France and Poland; Andrew Thevet." As for Espinosa's book, it does indeed give the information, but how Wordsworth acquired a rare sixteenth-century book in a language in which he does not seem to have been fluent and which (I am told) was not translated into English until 1907 as one of the Publications of the Hakluyt Society[6] — all these are unexplained by the commentators, who leave us with the picture of Wordsworth reading Plutarch in a

6. Havens, *The Mind of a Poet*, p. 296.

non-existent French translation and supplementing his information from a Spanish book which he was unlikely to possess and unlikely to be able to read with ease if he had possessed it. There is another account of this story, which gives all the significant details, including Plutarch on Sertorius, in an English work called *The History of the Discovery of the Canary Islands . . . By George Glas* (London, 1764), and which even provides a slight verbal parallel to one of Wordsworth's lines.[7] I do not know for certain that Wordsworth used this book; but it is a much more credible source, in my view, than Espinosa's. What moral do I draw? That commentators should, before they make rash proposals about Wordsworth's sources, check the information given in unreliable sale catalogues (this could have been done, in this instance, by a glance at the British Museum Catalogue), and consider the likelihood of Wordsworth obtaining information from a rare book which he could have read, if at all, only with difficulty.[8]

Sometimes the commentator must be armed with a knowledge of a particular jargon belonging to his author or to a period. Consider this summarizing passage in the latter part of *The Prelude*, Book I:

> Ye Presences of Nature, in the sky
> Or on the earth! Ye Visions of the hills!
> And Souls of lonely places! can I think
> A vulgar hope was yours when Ye employ'd
> Such ministry, when Ye through many a year
> Haunting me thus among my boyish sports,

7. *Prel.*, I.197-8: "when the European came/ With skill and power that could not be withstood"; Glas, pp. 64-65: "When the Europeans came first to Gran Canaria, that island was supposed to contain no less than fourteen thousand fighting men; but a great sickness or plague prevailing amongst them some time after, it swept away two thirds of the inhabitants."

8. In my paper as I read it I implied that Wordsworth knew little if any Spanish. Professor MacGillivray reminded me of two passages in early letters which indicate that Wordsworth might have had more Spanish than I allowed: "I regret much not having brought my Spanish Grammar along with me. By peeping into it occasionally I might perhaps have contrived to keep the little Spanish or some part of it, that I was master of . . . Of Spanish I have read none these three years" (*E.Y.*, pp. 56, 112; 3 August 1791, 17 February 1794). Glas's book still seems to me a more likely source.

> On caves and trees, upon the woods and hills,
> Impress'd upon all forms the characters
> Of danger or desire, and thus did make
> The surface of the universal earth
> With triumph, and delight, and hope, and fear,
> Work like a sea?
>
> (I.490-501)

I will not attempt to explicate the first three lines here, beyond observing that Wordsworth's use of the preposition *of* in such phrases deserves (in fact has had) study in an effort to discover just what genitival relation he has in mind.[9] I summarize roughly the drift of the early lines here by saying that various aspects of Nature are what "Impress'd upon all forms the characters/ Of danger or desire." But why "danger or desire"? The recurrence of this and similar doublets in the poem indicates to me that Wordsworth habitually thought of the natural scene (whether instinctively or from literary training) in terms of the contrasting concepts which the eighteenth century called the Sublime and the Beautiful.[10] Consider these passages from many; the most famous:

> Fair seed-time had my soul, and I grew up
> Foster'd alike by beauty and by fear
>
> (I.305-6)

– by the beautiful and the sublime. Or this:

> And not alone,
> In grandeur and in tumult, but no less
> In tranquil scenes, that universal power
> And fitness in the latent qualities
> And essences of things, by which the mind
> Is mov'd by feelings of delight, to me
> Came strengthen'd with a superadded soul,
> A virtue not its own.
>
> (II.341-8)

"Delight" goes with "tranquil scenes"; the contrasting passage, earlier, mentions walks by night "In storm and

---

9. Frances O. Austin, "Time, Experience and Syntax in Wordsworth's Poetry," *Neuphilologische Mitteilungen* 70, 1969, pp. 724-38.
10. Mr. Heffernan glances at this point (op. cit., pp. 156-60).

tempest, or in star-light nights/ Beneath the quiet Hea-
vens" (322-3), which produced "Sublimer joy" (321), "an
elevated mood" (325), "the visionary power" (330),
"shadowy exultation" (332), and

> an obscure sense
> Of possible sublimity, to which
> With growing faculties she [the soul] doth aspire,
> With faculties still growing, feeling still
> That whatsoever point they gain, they still
> Have something to pursue
>
> (II.336-41)

— a passage with which we need to compare a sentence in
the unpublished essay on the *Sublime and Beautiful*:
"Power awakens the sublime . . . when it rouses us to a
sympathetic energy & calls upon the mind to grasp at
something towards which it can make approaches but
which it is incapable of attaining" (*Prose*, II.354). Or this
passage from Book III:

> whatsoe'er of Terror or of Love,
> Or Beauty, Nature's daily face put on
> From transitory passion, unto this
> I was as wakeful, even, as waters are
> To the sky's motion.
>
> (III.132-6)

"Terror" goes with the sublime; "Love" or "Beauty"
makes the contrast.

In my original example, I propose that "danger" is
associated with the sublime, "desire" with the beautiful,
and that the emotions named two lines later (they are
attributed to "The surface of the universal earth," but
they must be transferred from the mind of the boy who
observed the earth) can likewise be associated with these
two categories: "delight"[11] and "hope" with beauty,
"fear" obviously with the sublime — what of "triumph"?

---

11. "Delight" is Burke's word, by his own defined usage, for "a species of
relative pleasure" arising from "the removal or moderation of pain"
(*Philosophical Enquiry*, Part I, Sect. IV), the connection of which with his
view of the Sublime is obvious. I do not think Wordsworth follows this usage,
as *Prel.*, II.346, cited above, indicates.

Triumph also with the sublime, for in his essay Wordsworth writes of this possible reaction to the sublime:

> there is no sublimity excited by the contemplation of power
> thought of as a thing to be resisted . . . saving only as far as the
> mind, either by glances or continuously, conceives that that
> power may be overcome or rendered evanescent, and as far as
> it feels itself tending toward the unity that exists in security or
> absolute triumph. (*Prose*, II, p. 356)

The alert commentator on my original passage will wish to
explicate "triumph, and delight, and hope, and fear"; he
will need to be well read in general eighteenth-century
aesthetics as well as in Wordsworth's own, in order to do
so adequately. In fact, no commentator on *The Prelude* so
troubles himself.

For a more significant example, let me revert to a
passage I cited before, the borrowing from *Paradise Lost*,
Book VII, in *The Prelude*, Book XIII:

> A hundred hills their dusky backs upheaved
> All over this still Ocean
>
> (XIII.45-46)

— the sea of mist at the summit of Snowdon;

> Immediately the Mountains huge appeer
> Emergent, and thir broad bare backs upheave
> Into the Clouds, thir tops ascend the Skie,

as Milton's God divides the land from the waters. This kind
of example is important because it raises the last point of
principle which is in my mind: how far does the
commentator regard himself as a literary critic? How far
does he go when he draws attention to a borrowing such as
this? Does he stop with a simple "Cf."? Or does he go on
to point out the splendid appropriateness of this reminiscence in these two passages dealing with creation — God's
in Milton, in Wordsworth Nature's, and Nature's then as an
emblem of the creativity of Man's imagination? Nature's,
and therefore Man's creative power as an echo of the
Divine Logos?

> God said . . .
> Immediately the Mountains huge appeer

> Emergent, and thir broad bare backs upheave
> Into the Clouds, thir tops ascend the Skie:
> So high as heav'd the tumid Hills, so low
> Down sunk a hollow bottom broad and deep,
> Capacious bed of Waters.

>   instantly a Light upon the turf
> Fell like a flash: I look'd about, and lo!
> The Moon stood naked in the Heavens, at height
> Immense above my head, and on the shore
> I found myself of a huge sea of mist,
> Which, meek and silent, rested at my feet:
> A hundred hills their dusky backs upheaved
> All over this still Ocean, and beyond,
> Far, far beyond, the vapours shot themselves,
> In headlands, tongues, and promontory shapes,
> Into the Sea, the real Sea . . .

>   (XIII.39-49)

"The perfect image of a mighty Mind" (69), says Wordsworth a little later, analogous to what he calls, later still in his discussion, "higher minds" (90), who mould the world into meaning, as Nature does in such visions and as God does in *Paradise Lost*. Is the commentator also a literary critic? Is his "Cf." sufficient? Perhaps it ought to be, if the reader takes the imperative seriously and actually places such a passage and its source side by side and sees what can be learned from the comparison or what richness of reminiscence can be extracted from it.

I began with the thesis that the commentary defines and defends the text, wherever the text is not self-evidently correct. This thesis I have modified and emended and supplemented as I have proceeded, first by showing that the commentary defends the text by drawing on linguistic evidence to demonstrate that the text is intelligible where the reader might have thought that it was not (and occasionally *vice versa*); then that the commentary defends the text by making it intelligible, not on grounds of mere logic or linguistic evidence, but by explicating the difficult factual reference; and from this version of my thesis I have moved, in my more recent examples, to the notion of the commentary as explicating the source, whether or not the

text is linguistically difficult, and whether by *source* one
means a passage verbally borrowed or adapted, or literary
or aesthetic ideas (or they might be philosophical or
psychological or political or whatever) on which the
author is relying and for which one could point to a *body*
of source-ideas rather than to a single work. And from that
idea of the commentary I have, in my last example, moved
to the idea of the commentary as the provider of basic
information for the literary critic.

For without the commentator who points out the
Miltonic echo in my last example, the critic cannot
function to his full potential. The commentator and the
critic may, of course, be the same man, as the textual
editor and the commentator may (indeed, in my view,
must) be the same man; and the critic does not need to
write down his formal "Cf." any more than does the
textual editor when the occasion does not require it. But
as, in Coleridge's view, genius must have talent, and
imagination must have fancy,[12] in order that genius and
imagination may function at all – so the critic must have
the commentator. Mr. Heffernan, whom I took to task for
his analysis of my last example, was, in this instance,
attempting to be a critic without first becoming a
commentator. Let me conclude with an instance where the
commentators, in my view, have even more grossly failed,
so that the critics have not begun to speak.

I shall discuss, not as fully as it deserves or as it can be
discussed, the famous opening passage of *The Prelude*, the
"glad preamble" (as Wordsworth calls it in a back-
reference at the beginning of Book VII), long discussed as
to its date of composition (which I hope is now firmly
fixed in 1799 by the late John Finch)[13] and its autobiographical veracity. I am not concerned with these matters,
but with the literary texture as the commentator may

12. *Table Talk*, 20 August 1833.
13. "Wordsworth's Two-Handed Engine," in *Bicentenary Wordsworth
Studies in Memory of John Alban Finch*, ed. Jonathan Wordsworth, Ithaca
and London, 1970, pp. 1-13.

assist the critic to expound it. I shall confine myself to the
first twenty lines or so of the passage, and I shall thrust
into the midst, beginning at line 15, where the commentators have indeed already been at work, observing that the
opening phrase of Wordsworth's line comes from *Paradise
Lost*:

> The earth is all before me: with a heart
> Joyous, nor scar'd at its own liberty,
> I look about, and should the guide I chuse
> Be nothing better than a wandering cloud,
> I cannot miss my way.
>
> (I.15-19)

"The World was all before them where to choose/ Thir
place of rest, and Providence thir guide," writes Milton of
Adam and Eve at the very end of *Paradise Lost*
(XII.646-7). Expand Wordsworth's borrowed phrase similarly, and we observe that the unborrowed words echo
Wordsworth's situation also: "where to choose/ Thir place
of rest" — this is his task, as this preamble to the poem
describes it. Adam and Eve, object the commentators, are
leaving Paradise for the world, Wordsworth is leaving the
world in search of Paradise. Not quite so: Eden is no
Paradise to Adam and Eve now, any more than London (or
whatever city he is leaving) is to Wordsworth at this time:
all are escaping from some kind of intellectual discomfort.
"Providence thir guide," says Milton; Wordsworth's guide
is "nothing better than a wandering cloud," less reliable,
one would think. Not so again: in the merely autobiographical context of this passage, Nature, by means of the
wandering cloud, is Providence. But for a wider context,
and a more meaningful one, look back a little:

> A captive greets thee [the breeze], coming from a house
> Of bondage, from yon City's walls set free.
>
> (I.6-7)

"House of bondage" is a biblical phrase, from Exodus
13:3: "Remember this day [as Wordsworth is doing], in
which ye came out from Egypt, out of the house of
bondage." So Wordsworth is made of the tribe of Israel,

seeking a new home after the captivity. "The World was all before them, where to choose/ Thir place of rest," for the Israelites as for Adam and Eve as for Wordsworth; "and Providence thir guide," to the Israelites as well as to Adam and Eve. And how did the Lord guide them in the wilderness, out of the house of bondage and towards the promised land? "And the Lord went before them by day in a pillar of a cloud, to lead them the way" (Exodus 13:21); "and should the guide I chuse/ Be nothing better than a wandering cloud,/ I cannot miss my way."

Observe how the bonuses of meaning, the richness of the texture, revealed by the commentator, build up, generalizing the individual poet William Wordsworth into Adam and Eve (all men *in potentia*) and the Israelites (great archetypes of Western Christian civilization) — God-guided all, setting out, all, for a new home, a new Paradise, a new promised land, "And Providence" (or a wandering cloud, it is the same thing) their guide to home, peace after stress, liberty after slavery. — Yet no commentator that I know troubles to record the biblical borrowings which hold the key to all this wealth of associative meaning.

I have pleaded the cause of the commentary as part of the editor's task. I plead, as Wordsworth himself did, for an accurate text; for the explication of difficulties in word and idea; for a knowledge of the poet's sources, so that we may know how he has used them — and for all these needs, in my view, the commentary, implicit or preferably explicit, as an essential aid. In short, I plead for the commentary as a means to a knowledge of the poet's knowledge, so that we may the better understand his art and his wisdom.

The Bentham Project

J. H. Burns

My position in this Conference might well be described in terms that are applicable to many sheets of Bentham manuscript: somewhat worn, rather obscure, and probably out of place. The case for my participation is, I suppose, that I can present the problems of editing texts of a radically different kind from the literary material with which most of you are concerned. There was, I believe, at one time a prospect of filling this slot in the programme with a scholar engaged in editing work in a modern foreign language. As to this, the best that can be said is that Jeremy Bentham, especially in later life, frequently wrote in a language which many would find it hard to accept as English. Idiosyncrasies of language and style, however, are only minor factors among those that differentiate the problems of editing Bentham from the equivalent problems in other cases. Every scholar engaged in editorial work, of course, will claim — and claim rightly — that the problems he or she faces are unique. This must in some sense be true in the nature of the case. Yet I hope to show that our problems with Bentham are, if not uniquely difficult, at least difficult in very special ways, to which few if any analogies can be found elsewhere.

There is, to begin with, the problem of size and scale. Bentham wrote with enormous energy and zeal for over sixty years. The earliest manuscripts we have – letters apart – appear to date from about 1770, when Bentham was twenty-two. The latest to survive bear dates only a few months before his death at the age of eighty-four in 1832. Of these labours, the published product, in the extensive but incomplete collection which has hitherto been the standard edition of Bentham's works,[1] fills nine large volumes, some 5,500 pages in double columns of painfully small print – representing a total of perhaps 11,000,000 words. And that edition, as I have said, is incomplete. It omits, for example, all Bentham's writings on religious and ecclesiastical topics – which are expected to fill four substantial volumes in the comprehensive edition now projected. Nor does the Bowring edition represent either fully or accurately all that is to be found in the surviving mass of Bentham's manuscripts. Of these, the principal collection is in the library of University College London: it comprises, very roughly, 60,000 sheets. To this must be added the British Museum's substantial holding of Bentham material, which fills over thirty volumes in the Manuscript Department. In the Dumont Collection in Geneva there is further relevant manuscript material, while the scatter of Bentham correspondence (and other items) has already taken our search from the Soviet Union to the Pacific shores of the United States, with many unresolved problems in between: what, for instance, has become of the substantial parcels of *Constitutional Code* manuscript which Bentham sent to Greece at the period of the national liberation struggle there?

1. *The Works of Jeremy Bentham, published under the superintendence of his executor, John Bowring*, 11 vols., Edinburgh, 1838-43: vols. I-IX comprise Bentham's works, vols. X and XI Bowring's Memoirs of Bentham together with an elaborate index to the collection compiled by John Hill Burton. Burton (1809-81), later Historiographer Royal of Scotland, was responsible for most of the real editorial work on what is commonly called "the Bowring edition."

From scale it is logical to turn to scope and range. The editorial problems in dealing with such a mass of material would be formidable enough if the material itself fell into a single category or into a relatively small number of categories. But Bentham's mind, though limited — even perversely so — in certain directions, was wide-ranging. The subjects on which he wrote — penology, procedure, and political economy would be no more than a small alliterative sample — have in most cases since his time developed into highly specialised disciplines or branches of knowledge. To edit Bentham's works properly thus requires the co-operation of scholars in many different fields, and the scholars in question must combine with expertise in their subjects awareness of the historical and intellectual circumstances in which Bentham wrote and sensitivity to the demands of editorial technique. These problems are not made easier by the fact that Bentham (in love throughout his life with the notion of systematic exposition of interrelated subjects, but incapable of consummating the wished-for marriage) wrote works that overlapped and intertwined with one another in a way that makes it enormously hard to work to a plan based on vertical divisions between different subjects. How is one to deal, for instance, with a discussion of nomenclature and classification which belongs to Bentham's scheme for "chrestomathic" education and yet has the most obvious of links with his extensive but unfinished writings on language and logic? Or with an extensive unpublished work on the emancipation of the Spanish and Portuguese colonies in Latin America which follows the essentially economic arguments against colonisation deployed in *Emancipate Your Colonies!* but goes on to develop political and constitutional arguments to the extent that some of the manuscripts were subsequently reheaded for Bentham's *Constitutional Code*?

The issues just raised take us from the problems associated with the range of Bentham's interests to those deriving from the character of his writings in general and the ways in which they were published during his lifetime and immediately afterward.

I have referred already to a fundamental paradox in Bentham's work: the lifelong ambition to create a systematic body of doctrine and the persistent failure to make real progress towards such a system. A specific instance of this will serve to illustrate the editorial problems it creates. Bentham's intended system involved from an early stage the writing of a penal code as one of its elements. On this he made a substantial start in the late 1770s; but the work was left unfinished, and only the Introduction to his *Plan of a Penal Code* was ever published – as *An Introduction to the Principles of Morals and Legislation*.[2] Half a century later, however, Bentham was still committed to the production of a penal code – an elaborate table of its intended contents was published in Volume I of his *Constitutional Code* in 1830. As a result we have two groups of manuscripts, separated by fifty years yet in some sense designed for the same part of Bentham's comprehensive system of legislation. Nor can we assume that Bentham would himself have simply discarded the early material. He did this sometimes, of course. But it was characteristic of him to go back again and again to manuscripts written years before and to consider their availability for present projects. Such manuscripts may be redated, reheaded, renumbered several times over, revised and marked in all kinds of ways. All this, combined with the increasingly villainous character of Bentham's handwriting, obviously accentuates the difficulties faced by an editor.

Yet those problems would matter less than they do had Bentham's writings followed anything like an orthodox course from original draft through subsequent revisions to publication, under the author's eye and with his approval, of finished works. In fact this course was hardly ever followed. It is extraordinarily hard to point to any major

2. Ed. J. H. Burns and H. L. A. Hart (1970) in *The Collected Works of Jeremy Bentham*, London, 1968-.

work which was published in this way in Bentham's lifetime. This brings us to a further peculiarity in the problems with which any modern edition of Bentham has to deal. Not only did Bentham encounter insuperable obstacles in the way of completing his overall system. He suffered also from an almost total inability to complete even single works of any substance for publication. There were evidently psychological factors at work here, no doubt related to those which in other contexts led Bentham to fight shy of opportunities which, before the event, he regarded as desirable – his reluctance, for instance, to meet Shelburne until the meeting was all but forced on him by the great man himself.[3] There was also, clearly, some degree of obsessive perfectionism – reflected again in the manuscripts, with their constant rewriting, revision, and reordering. At the same time Bentham seems to have drawn from a remarkably early age the conclusion that the genius for legislation which he had tremblingly recognised in himself at the age of twenty-one, could find expression only if he had coadjutors. Surprisingly soon he began to think of these helpers as "disciples" rather than simply collaborators. John Lind, with whom Bentham worked closely in the 1770s,[4] could not be cast for the subordinate role; but Bentham was in due course to attract a number of remarkable followers who were prepared, for a time at least, to submit their own not inconsiderable talents to the exacting discipline of preparing Bentham's intractable and increasingly voluminous manuscripts for the public.

In a group which included notable personalities like James and John Stuart Mill, George Grote and Francis Place, together with lesser figures like Peregrine Bingham and Richard Smith ("of the Stamps and Taxes"),[5] the

3. See The Correspondence of Jeremy Bentham, in Collected Works: vol. II, ed. T. L. S. Sprigge, (1968), esp. pp. 470-1 and n.; vol. III, ed. I. R. Christie (1971), esp. pp. 24 ff. and n.
4. For Lind (1737-81) see Correspondence, vols. I and II, ed. Sprigge, (1968), passim.
5. James and John Stuart Mill are further referred to below. Grote edited

outstanding place belongs necessarily to Etienne Dumont of Geneva.[6] Dumont first made Bentham's acquaintance in the Shelburne circle; but it was not until he was again in England as a refugee from revolutionary France, where he had played a notable part in Mirabeau's *"atelier"* that he took up in earnest a task which was to occupy him off and on for over thirty years. This was to extract from what Bentham himself already called the "chaos" of his manuscripts a series of works which, published in French and beginning in 1802 with the *Traités de législation civile et pénale*, virtually established Bentham as a significant thinker with a substantial reputation. This is true not only in respect of his standing in Europe, though Dumont's versions circulated widely there both in the original French and in translations into other languages (notably Spanish). It is true also of Bentham's own country. Apart from the considerable success of his *Defence of Usury* (1787) Bentham, who was over fifty years of age before the eighteenth century ended, had made little impact on English intellectual life. His emergence as a figure in that world may perhaps be dated from the notice taken of Dumont's *Traités* in the recently established *Edinburgh Review* and elsewhere. Yet the Dumont works, substantially Benthamic no doubt, were not Bentham's own; and when it is realised that some of the English texts through which Bentham's ideas became most familiar later in the century were in fact retranslations from Dumont's French,[7] the peculiar complexities of the case will be apparent.

I have been trying to identify some of the major factors which constitute the special editorial problems connected

---

An Analysis of the Influence of Natural Religion ... (1822) from Bentham's MSS, while Place was concerned in the editing of, among other items, *Chrestomathia* (1815, 1816). Bingham edited *The Book of Fallacies* (1824), Smith, *The Rationale of Reward* (1825) and *The Rationale of Punishment* (1830). (Smith was also to collaborate extensively in the Bowring edition of Bentham's *Works*).

6. Pierre Etienne Louis Dumont (1759-1829).

7. The outstanding instance is *The Theory of Legislation*, the work of Richard Hildreth (1807-65), first published at Boston in 1840.

with Bentham's writings. To present a less abstract picture, however, it seems useful to expound some specific examples in rather more detail. For this purpose I have selected three works, one from each of what may be regarded as the early, the middle, and the late periods of Bentham's career.

In 1783 or thereabouts Bentham embarked on a new concept of the systematic treatise which he had by then had it in mind to write for over a dozen years. For reasons which need not in detail concern us here but which seem to have been connected with problems and disappointments he had experienced in securing suitable translations of his work for presentation to influential European readers, he decided this time to write the work in French himself.[8] It was to bear some such title as *Projet d'un corps complet de droit*, and was designed to comprise two principal parts. The first was to expound the *Forme* – the formal structure and logical interdependence of the whole code and its several parts; the second was to be concerned with the *Matière*, the substantive content of the various divisions into which the code would fall. That Bentham failed to complete this enterprise may now go almost without saying. What he did virtually complete was the *Forme* part of the *Projet*; and the manuscripts for this were subsequently used by Dumont for that part of his 1802 *Traités* which bore the subtitle *Vue générale d'un corps complet de droit*. Dumont's version is, as usual, a much chastened recension of Bentham's original, the chastening process here including a considerable purification of Bentham's fluent but idiosyncratic French. When in due course the Bowring edition of Bentham's work was being prepared, a straight retranslation of Dumont entitled *A General View of a Complete Code of Law*[9] was incorporated. Since the manuscript basis for all this survives in a reasonably coherent state, our task here, though complex in detail, is simple in essence; we must

8. See *Correspondence*, vol. III, ed. Christie, p. 151 and n., etc.
9. Bowring edn., vol. III, pp. 155-210.

and shall restore the original Bentham text of this part of the *Projet*. When we turn to the second part, however, the *Matière*, the situation is different. Here again we find substantial groups of manuscript material. But, on the one hand, there are large gaps, parts of the work which seem never to have been written at all; and, further, those parts that do survive seem to have grown under Bentham's hands, as so often happened, in such a way as to lead him eventually to the conclusion that separate works on the subjects in question would have to be written.[10] The substantive part of the *Projet* is thus at once defective and superabundant, and much manuscript originally written for this purpose can now most sensibly be regarded as material associated with the separate works to which it eventually gave rise. This will inevitably mean, however, that material originally written by Bentham at one period and for a single systematic purpose, will appear in different and perhaps in widely separated parts of our edition.

My example from Bentham's middle period is his massive work (or works) on evidence. Bentham had devoted some attention to this topic from quite an early stage in his career, but the great body of manuscript which confronted John Stuart Mill when, in 1825, he began the editorial labours that were to yield the five-volume *Rationale of Judicial Evidence* in 1827, was (as Mill himself tells us) the product of three several attempts by Bentham to write a treatise on the subject. One of these attempts had indeed made substantial progress towards publication with the help of James Mill. A considerable part of what was not in fact to be published until its appearance in vol. VI of the Bowring edition as *An Introductory View of the Rationale of Evidence* was printed in or about 1812. A dozen years later Bentham himself went back to this material and put in order the

---

10. A notable instance of this "growing" process is the continuation of the unfinished Chap. XVII of *An Introduction to the Principles of Morals and Legislation*, which eventually became the separate treatise published in *Collected Works* as *Of Laws in General*, ed. H. L. A. Hart (1970).

manuscripts for the part of the work not yet printed. The stimulus for this seems to have been the appearance in 1823 of yet another Dumont recension. The evidence manuscripts had been transmitted to Dumont and he had published one of his masterly distillations as *Traité des preuves judiciaires*. This in turn was anonymously translated into English and published in 1825 as *A Treatise on Judicial Evidence*. We do not as yet know to what extent Bentham himself was privy to and in favour of this translation project; but his lack of complete satisfaction at least seems to be evinced by his having commissioned John Mill just about this time to prepare the much more comprehensive treatise published in 1827. Bentham's general approval of the younger Mill's work is well established; yet there is also evidence, recently discovered, that he had amendments to suggest, at least in detail, after its publication.[11]

We encounter in this case, therefore, a complex of printed works and manuscript material, among which it is extremely hard to determine what is to be regarded as definitive. As in other cases we are reliving problems faced by earlier editors; for correspondence surviving from the 1830s shows uncertainty and disagreement over the policy to be adopted in respect of the works on evidence in the Bowring edition. That the *Introductory View*, the one work which Bentham himself seems to have been largely concerned in bringing to a state fit for publication should reappear as it stands seems clear. The J. S. Mill text of the *Rationale* has manifest authority; but on present evidence it seems that we lack the actual manuscript basis from which Mill worked, so that we cannot precisely identify and evaluate the editorial changes he made, apart from those to which he himself drew attention. At the same time we have a large body of manuscript material which corresponds in varying senses and degrees to what is in

---

11. Much of this paragraph is based on recent research by Dr. F. Rosen, Assistant General Editor of the project, and by Professor W. L. Twining of the University of Warwick (formerly of the Queen's University of Belfast).

print. If we are not to print all of it *in extenso* – and to do so would, apart from any other problems, create great areas of what would substantially be repetition in a field which already accounts for two whole volumes (VI and VII) in the Bowring edition – careful editorial decisions will be required as to which parts are to be printed and what kind of attention is to be paid to the rest.

Finally I come to the major work of Bentham's later years, the *Constitutional Code*. After slightly ambiguous hesitations in his earliest years as a writer Bentham had, from the beginning of the 1780s at least, recognised that constitutional law must form an important part of any system such as he envisaged. But he did not devote any sustained attention to it until, in the early 1820s, a number of events in the political world prompted him to draft such a code "for all nations professing liberal opinions." Spain and Portugal, their recently emancipated colonies, and the Greek struggle for national independence in turn fostered Bentham's interest in this project. As a result he had made by 1823-24 substantial progress towards completing a comprehensive system of constitutional arrangements. A "trailer" had even appeared in print, as *Leading Principles of a Constitutional Code* (1823) – the first of a number of pre-published extracts which bedevil a bibliographical situation which would be complex enough without them. By 1827, the first nine chapters of a revised and compressed version of the *Code* were in print; but not until three years later did Bentham decide to publish these in the first of three projected volumes. He had by then, with considerable help from associates with specialised knowledge, written the immense tenth chapter on the defensive force of the state. This too was printed, but not published; and so far as can be ascertained only one copy of that printing survives – in the Library of Congress. For these ten chapters, then, we have a printed text sealed with Bentham's approval (though far from typographically impeccable); and, as usually happens when Bentham had prevailed upon himself to go thus far, the manuscript on which the printed text was based is no longer extant. But the *Constitutional Code* was to have thirty-two chapters, and for the twenty-two that were not printed in Bentham's lifetime the work of putting together the text from the manuscript material was left undone at Bentham's death. The text of this part of the work as it appeared for the first time in the ninth volume of the Bowring edition (1841) had had a chequered history. The first steps had been taken, it seems, by Arthur Moore, who was Bentham's secretary at the time of his death. Edwin Chadwick, however, who as a young member of the Bentham workshop had himself worked on the drafting of the *Code*, weighed Moore's work and found it wanting. The demands on Chadwick's time in the 1830s, however, were not such as to allow of his becoming an active collaborator in the Bowring edition. After considerable delay and with some reluctance, Richard Doane, another of Bentham's former secretaries, who had already prepared Bentham's material on procedure for the edition, undertook the daunting task of completing the *Constitutional Code* from the manuscripts. To this end he did two things. First, he edited text for the twenty-two chapters envisaged in Bentham's plan but not reduced to final form before his death. Second, Doane put together from a large body of more or less relevant material an introductory discussion of constitutional problems which appears as Book I in his edition. In both contexts he left aside considerable quantities of manuscript, some, but by no means all, of which had been marked by Bentham as "superseded," but much of which adds to the substance and detail of Bentham's argument, some of it incidentally representing later work than the manuscripts Doane chose to use.

Here is another complex situation for editorial treatment. For about half the substantive *Code* we have a printed text authorised by Bentham and virtually no manuscript basis. For the remainder, and for the general discourse which Bentham had hoped to preface to the whole, we have printed texts which represent the often thoroughly reasonable decisions of an editor who had been Bentham's secretary and whose work one can often only admire and follow. His decisions, however, need not always and sometimes cannot be endorsed. We must do our own work of reconstruction on the text where Bentham had not finally approved it. And in the mass of alternative versions and associated material we expect to find enough and to spare for a third volume to set beside the two in which our text of the substantive *Code* will appear. There may even be a possibility of, and a case for, reconstructing in something like its complete state the *Constitutional Code* in its first definitive form, as Bentham wrote it in 1823 and 1824. But here, as in the case of the evidence material, it would seem visionary rather than practical to attempt to reproduce all the manuscript. When one is committed to something like forty volumes – and, I sometimes think, to as many years' work – the prospect of adding still further volumes for the purpose of incorporating varied but substantially identical restatements of the same themes is one that cannot easily be accepted.

What I have said about my three examples will have indicated much of what I want to say about the nature and scope of the new edition. We have already been taken to task for not producing a totally complete variorum edition. Such an enterprise has of course a certain grandeur about it; and in one sense to print all that Bentham wrote, together with all the versions made by others out of what he wrote, would be an easier task than the one we have in fact undertaken. There may, indeed, be parts of the manuscript material which, because they defy any possible attempt to present them in coherent order, must be printed as they stand – the long series of disjointed and serially numbered paragraphs, for instance, in which Bentham wrote down ideas for what he then, in the 1770s, called his *Preparatory Principles*. But applied to the whole edition this approach would surely be, if I may so put it, a *grandeur de folie*. Not only are there limits, as we all know, to funds for research and publication, and limits to the available manpower and mental energy. There are limits to the real usefulness of such undertakings, a law of diminishing returns to be heeded here as elsewhere.

If the Bentham project is ever completed, if the forty volumes of which I have spoken ever in fact stand ranged upon library shelves, what will they provide which does not now exist and which the world of scholarship may find to be of some service? Well, to begin where our publishing programme itself began, with an aspect of the project to which I have made little or no reference so far, the edition will include the first comprehensive collection of Bentham's correspondence. Three volumes published so far have taken us to the autumn of 1788; the fourth volume, which is in an advanced stage of preparation, and the fifth, on which the work of transcription has made a substantial start, will take us, perhaps, eighteen or twenty years further. At least a further three volumes will be required to complete the series. If little has been said of this aspect of the project it is not because I underrate its importance. It is indeed one of the most important parts of the whole edition and will make available more fully than ever before biographical data which are essential to any proper assessment of Bentham's life, personality, and achievement. But the editorial problems here are, unlike those we encounter in Bentham's works, broadly similar to those faced in any such edition. There are the same frustrating gaps in what survives and the same questions to be resolved as to the extent to which in-letters should be printed and the degree of annotation that is appropriate. And there will eventually be – for someone, but (I venture to hope) not for me – the problem of preparing the analytical index to the whole correspondence which is to supplement the indexes of names of persons which are appearing volume by volume.

In the thirty or more volumes which will comprise the remainder of the edition, what we shall hope to provide is, first and foremost, a series of texts as to whose authenti-

city there will be no doubt. Hitherto, for reasons I have
tried to indicate, the published texts of Bentham's works
have, in many cases, been variously derived from his
original manuscripts in ways that must leave the informed
reader in doubt as to whether, in any given passage, he is
or is not reading what Bentham wrote and meant. Every
text we publish will represent primarily either what
Bentham himself approved for publication or what is to be
found in his own manuscripts. With this we shall of course
endeavour to provide such editorial apparatus as will
exhibit the relationship between these texts and what have
so far been the received versions. We shall print as fully as
circumstances allow the various alternative versions which
Bentham left. For reasons already indicated, however, this
edition will not include, in the terms once ambitiously
used for a one-volume Shakespeare, "everything Bentham
ever wrote." We have deliberately eschewed the word
"complete" in our title. Yet in one important sense the
edition will be a complete collection of Bentham's works.
It will include, that is to say, everything, whether
previously printed or not, which can meaningfully be
termed "a work"; and it will also include whatever
fragmentary materials seem to the editors to embody
material of substantial interest and importance.

I do not feel any need to apologise for the element of
editorial discretion which is necessarily involved in what
has just been said. The enterprise in which we are engaged
would, I suggest, move from the realm of the extremely
difficult to that of the totally impossible if such discretion
were not to be exercised. We shall of course draw attention
to the existence and, at least in general terms, to the
character of what we do not print. There will still be work
for the minute scholar to do on the Bentham papers when
− if − our edition reaches completion. This may perhaps
be good news for generations of Ph.D. students yet
unregistered, if not unborn.

Editorial discretion is involved *en détail* as well as *en
gros*. Just as we cannot, in my judgment, reproduce every

version of every work on which Bentham embarked, so we cannot, in the texts we do publish, present anything like a facsimile in print of manuscripts which are, to put it mildly, more than ordinarily complex and obscure. In publishing the essentially personal documentation of the *Correspondence* section of the edition, we are indeed preserving nearly every idiosyncrasy. But in publishing Bentham's works we have felt it to be both necessary and desirable to interpose some degree of editorial filtering between the reader and the harsh reality of manuscripts which, in all but a few cases, cannot be regarded as representing what would have been Bentham's final copy for the press. This involves, above all, editorial choice between — or among — purely verbal variants; and our general principle here is to prefer wherever possible what appears to have been Bentham's latest revision. Alternative readings will be recorded wherever it seems possible that any substantial difference of meaning might be involved. At this level, however, as at the more macroscopic level of alternative versions of substantial passages of text, the concept of a full-scale variorum edition does not appear to be practicable. I would not wish to claim that in the one work so far published of which the basis lies in manuscript material rather than in earlier printed texts (*Of Laws in General*), we have achieved a totally satisfactory solution of these and the many cognate problems that are involved. But I would hope that with over thirty volumes to go we shall rapidly refine our techniques and perfect our presentation; and I should like to think that the five volumes published between 1968 and 1971, whatever defects they may have in detail, represent as a whole a solid justification of what we are trying to do and of the ways in which we are trying to do it.

On Editing Coleridge's Marginalia

George Whalley

When I accepted your kind invitation to address this learned gathering, I had never been to a conference of literary editors before and wondered what like it would be, and consulted my colleagues. Was a literary editor like the ant-eater, I asked, because of his long swift tongue, and those powerful claws of his that can quickly tear open the toughest anthill, and because he also, in the fur of his back, seems to wear an academic hood? Or was he more like the road-runner, or the giraffe, in whom there is so little relation between the speed of the footwork and the grave and steady forward movement of the head? No one figure, they said, would serve; literary editors are too select a race, each too peculiar to his own task to submit to Linnaen classification or the elevated moralizings of Buffon. Fortunately Coleridge was a self-condemned "Mottophilist": there I might begin, with a motto; or rather two: with George Leigh Mallory's answer to the question why he wanted to climb a mountain — "Because it's *there*," and a legendary piece of advice for cooking a hare — "First catch your hare."

To edit the text of the notes Coleridge wrote in the

margins and on the flyleaves of his own and other people's books is presumably no different from editing any text that was informally and spontaneously written and was not intended or prepared for publication. A conclusion depends upon the premisses it stands on, but it is also the case that the premisses are profoundly affected by the preliminary glimpse one has of a possible conclusion. So it may help to start in the natural way at the beginning, and — if need be — to be shamelessly a little autobiographical. For my work on the Coleridge marginalia has suffered from an obliquity truly Coleridgean, and is therefore in some sense its own argument.

Late in 1945, when I was no longer required (as the 37th Article of Religion has it) "to wear weapons, and serve in the wars," I was able to turn to a matter that had long occupied my thoughts: to examine — and if possible to delineate — various functions of the human mind. Because it is difficult to correlate one function in one mind with another function in another mind, I had decided to try to find — if such existed — a large body of informal and spontaneous writing by one person whose mental activities were many-sided and whose achievement in each sphere of activity was unquestionably of a high order. I need not rehearse the possibilities that presented themselves; the specification was a rather refined one and the choice eventually — perhaps inevitably — settled on Coleridge without any guess at what was involved. It was an open choice in the sense that I was in no sense a Coleridge specialist — or even a literary specialist — and had no intention of being a scholar; my acquaintance with Coleridge was limited to the poems, those parts of the canon that every literate person sooner or later reads, and John Livingston Lowes's *The Road to Xanadu* which I had consumed with excitement as an undergraduate some twelve years earlier. Knowing that a number of manuscript notebooks existed in the possession of the Coleridge family, and that a number of annotated books and a quantity of miscellaneous manuscript were preserved in

the British Museum and elsewhere, I set about to find out
what was what and what was where, and very soon had the
good fortune to meet Miss Kathleen Coburn and to find
that her work of editing the notebooks had already been
under way for ten years or more. I turned therefore to
consider Coleridge's reading and the written record of his
response to what he read (with a good deal of help and
generous assistance from Miss Coburn).

Clearly it would be some years before the materials for a
study of the growth and activity of Coleridge's mind
would be in manageable condition. While making a
preliminary inquiry into the question whether it was in
fact possible to investigate another mind without simply
finding projected there the patterns of what one wanted to
find — (I concluded that it might be just possible; that
inquiry was called *Poetic Process*) — I set about accumu-
lating as much information as possible about what Coleridge had read, and when, and (if possible) why — and
what he had done with the reading. The relation to my
original intention is clear: as in Lowes's *Road to Xanadu*,
the study of the reading was to be, not a study of
Coleridge's sources and "influences," but of his findings,
soundings, and transformations. Beyond the purpose I had
intended, I thought that if it were thoroughly done, and if
one were lucky in matters of chronology, this compilation
might help to identify and date some of the problematical
entries in the Coleridge notebooks, and would provide
clarifying and expository evidence for editing the canoni-
cal works — whoever was going to edit them. The first
annotated list of reading was based on a study of
Coleridge's books and manuscripts preserved in the British
Museum and upon lists and descriptions of annotated
books and manuscripts in the possession of the Coleridge
family (accessible at that time only to Kathleen Coburn),
and amplified by a search of the published works of
Coleridge and of his friends, associates, and acquaintances,
library borrowing registers, and sale catalogues. The
Department of Veterans' Affairs, and the pretext of a

doctorate (for in those days it was a matter of "no degree-project, no cash"), enabled me to spend two years in England preparing my first document on Coleridge's reading (*S. T. Coleridge: Library Cormorant*, 2 vols type-script, London, 1950) which my supervisor Professor Geoffrey Bullough ruefully described as about the size of two London telephone directories. Whether the account of some 1,100 titles, with descriptive and critical commentary, was in fact an Appendix to the introductory mental biography, or the biographical essay a suggestive introduction to the Reading List, is a nice question that Coleridge himself might have savoured with a twinge of recognition, and left unanswered. I have held ever since to the figure of Coleridge as a cormorant, not so much for his voracious appetite as for his flawless digestion.

At that stage it was necessary to work with some detailed precision in identifying, locating, and describing the books that Coleridge had owned or written in or that had passed through his hands; but the text of the marginalia was not matter of primary concern in preparing *Cormorant*. I did however transcribe marginalia whenever I could find the originals and had included what I took to be a characteristic selection of these in the descriptive and critical commentary. At that time – and indeed for several years – there seemed little likelihood that the text of *all* the marginalia could be published because of their extent, and because the specialised and obscure nature of many of the notes would demand a layer of detailed commentary that would certainly be expected to repel both the "general reader" and the most disinterested of scholarly publishers. But the tide of Coleridge scholarship had already set much more strongly than I had guessed; and after the notebooks and a splendid group of annotated books had been placed in the British Museum in 1951, and in 1954 the other major Coleridge family collection of manuscripts and books had been acquired by Victoria College, Toronto – both as a result of Kathleen Coburn's energetic imagination (or imaginative energy) – it was only a matter of time, and not a very long time, before the long-cherished project for a collected edition of Coleridge works – again through Miss Coburn's initiative – became a reality under the sponsorship of the Bollingen Foundation. I put aside the refined and amplified version of "The Old *Cormorant*" that I had been working at, and accepted Kathleen Coburn's invitation to prepare an edition of all the marginalia for the *Collected Coleridge* edition. In this form the edition is now being completed, and is expected to make four volumes or so in the *Collected Works*.

EXTENT OF THE MARGINALIA

It is not appropriate on this occasion to argue the importance of the marginalia, or to offer a conspective account of them, or to discuss why Coleridge wrote in the margins of his books, or to wonder whether in fact any English writer has left behind such a quantity of notes written in printed books; nor is it necessary to consider the relation between the marginalia and Coleridge's other work, except to say that he himself regarded many of the marginalia as an important part of his canon, and that he hoped to extract and arrange them for publication, and that when he realised he would not be able to do that, he evidently did not refrain from instructing his earliest editors – his nephew Henry Nelson Coleridge and his daughter Sara (HNC's wife). They began their work immediately after Coleridge's death, and by the time they had finished their work in 1853, marginalia represented more than a third of all Coleridge's published prose work. Yet (for reasons that need not be considered here) marginalia in whole categories of books – particularly philosophical, scientific, and biblical works – had not been published, and few of the sets of marginalia that had been published were complete. Of the 305 titles of association books listed by John Louis Haney in 1903 (some of which were not then accessible) less than 90 titles had been used by the family editors. It is now possible to bring together marginalia from almost 450 titles (by more than 350 authors) and to add to these some 150 titles of books known to have been annotated which are now lost (though some or all the notes in about half the lost books are preserved in some form or other); and to add more than 400 titles of "marked books" — that is, books in which Coleridge wrote his name or which bear a presentation inscription to or by him. Though the marked books provide no marginalia, they offer indispensable evidence for readings — both before and after the beginning of profuse annotation in about 1804 — which are known from other witnesses to have been important to him. The extent of marginalia is not always a mark of relative importance to Coleridge: many books that were of first importance to him are not annotated at all.

The amount of annotation is very variable: quite a number of books have only one or two notes; the most heavily annotated — Jeremy Taylor's *Polemicall Discourses* (1674, folio) — has 259 notes. The notes themselves also vary widely in length, from a single word or a pregnant question mark to a small essay that may fill up two or more blank folio pages, or run head-and-foot through ten or twelve openings of an amply margined octavo. At the latest statistical round-up of marginalia for which we have a text, there were slightly less than 8000 single notes. There are 350 notes on the four surviving copies of Shakespeare's works; two copies of Richard Baxter's *Reliquiae Baxterianae* provide 172 notes; there is a total of 170 notes on Schelling, 116 on Kant, 141 on Tennemann's *Geschichte der Philosophie*, nearly 200 on various biblical commentaries of Eichhorn's (all unpublished); the 93 notes on three copies of Robert Leighton's *Works* record the initial shock of self-recognition and the growth — through ten years — of these notes into *Aids to Reflection*; the numerous notes on Marcus Aurelius's *Meditations* and on Luther's *Colloquia Mensalia* are a curious blend of theological and philosophical reflection and of unflinching personal introspection. Although some books are lightly annotated and the description can be quite brief, others

Coleridge note in ink on Boehme

The Works of Jacob Behmen (4 vols., London 1764-1781),
vol. I, part i, p. [23].

Written in the spring of 1808, typically in ink and
perfectly legible, the note has already run through the
preceding blank page and concludes on the next page. The
leaves are uncut and all the writing is intact. (British
Museum C.126.k.1; reproduced by permission of the
Trustees.)

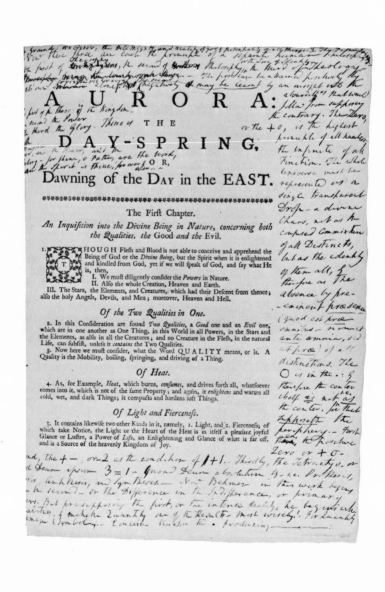

A U R O R A:

THE
DAY-SPRING,
OR,
Dawning of the Day in the EAST.

The First Chapter.

*An Inquisition into the Divine Being in Nature, concerning both
the Qualities, the Good and the Evil.*

1. THOUGH Flesh and Blood is not able to conceive and apprehend the Being of God or the *Divine Being*, but the Spirit when it is enlightened and kindled from God, yet if we will speak of God, and say what He is, then,

I. We must diligently consider the *Powers* in Nature.

II. Also the whole Creation, Heaven and Earth.

III. The Stars, the Elements, and Creatures, which had their Descent from thence; also the holy Angels, Devils, and Men; moreover, Heaven and Hell.

Of the Two Qualities in One.

2. In this Consideration are found *Two Qualities*, a *Good* one and an *Evil* one; which are in one another as One Thing, in this World in all Powers, in the Stars and the Elements, as also in all the Creatures; and no Creature in the Flesh, in the natural Life, can subsist, unless it *contains* the Two Qualities.

3. Now here we must consider, what the Word QUALITY means, or is. A Quality is the Mobility, boiling, springing, and driving of a Thing.

Of Heat.

4. As, for Example, *Heat*, which burns, *consumes*, and drives forth all, whatsoever comes into it, which is not of the same Property; and again, it *enlightens* and warms all cold, wet, and dark Things; it compacts and hardens soft Things.

Of Light and Fierceness.

5. It contains likewise two other Kinds in it, namely, 1. Light, and 2. Fierceness; of which take Notice, the Light or the Heart of the Heat is in itself a pleasant joyful Glance or Lustre, a Power of *Life*, an Enlightening and Glance of what is far off, and is a Source of the heavenly Kingdom of Joy.

need rather elaborate presentation. The printer's copy for
the single entry for William Law's edition of *The Works of
Jacob Behmen* (4 vols 4°, London, 1764-81), for example
— comprising a General Note on Coleridge's acquaintance
with Boehme's work and his critical response to it, a
description of the volumes, with an account of the
provenance of the volumes and of the dating of single
notes, the textus and MS of the 177 marginalia, and the
necessary footnotes by way of elucidation — runs to 220
pages of typescript. A large proportion of the marginalia
either have never been published, or have been published
incomplete and sometimes in a text blurred by the desire
to make authoritative and public what was intimate and
heuristic, or to make respectable what was in its concep-
tion daring and even disrespectful. The quantity and
intricacy of the materials present problems of housekeeping, but housekeeping is, like women's work, never
done; anyway it is part of an editor's job so I will say no
more of it.

<h2 style="text-align:center">TEXT AND ARRANGEMENT</h2>

The presentation of marginalia in printed form has always
raised difficulties and has never been satisfactorily resolved
except possibly in those fifteenth-century biblical commentaries where a fragment of primary text is placed
squarely in the type area and the various orders of notes
cluster and constellate around it, in various sizes and
characters, according to the peculiar demands of each
lemma of text and the learned whims of the editor. With
such an arrangement an approach to a diplomatic or
type-facsimile production could be contemplated; but for
such a lay-out (these days) at least double typesetting
would be needed and the prospect of the printer's bills
takes the wind out of the sails of even the most
luxuriously disinterested bibliomaniac. For Coleridge himself the sheer restriction of margins, the accidental
disposition of blank spaces, flytitles, and flyleaves, and his
need to write (from preference) at the site of the text that

had initiated reflection — these are all part of the shaping resistance that make the marginalia distinctively what they are; and the fact that he wrote his marginal notes in ink from choice (except in the German books where the "spongy Goodwin sands" of unsized paper would leave any ink-notes, as he said, "Wrecks hulling shapeless in the Margins") gives a hint of the devil-may-care sure-footedness of his attack. To lose in a printed version the pressure and hazard of those physical restraints is to a great extent to lose the sense of the impetuous gravity of the writing, the élan of the "shaping spirit of Imagination." For a large edition, however, a typefacsimile would defeat its own purpose by drawing attention to physical oddities that are not consonant with the writing. A number of reproductions of typical pages and openings dispersed through the edition can keep in the reader's mind's eye the look of the originals.

Again, although the marginalia seldom confine their discourse simply or strictly to the printed text they are associated with (though quite often they do), it is essential to see either what in the printed text is being referred to or what in the printed text has set his mind dreaming. (I settled finally upon the monkish word *textus* — plural *textūs* — to refer to that portion of the printed text to which a marginal note refers or with which it is associated; and incidentally the singular of *marginalia* is — as Coleridge knew — *marginale*). Editors of marginalia have always recognised the need to provide textus; but the typographical presentation of textus and MS together raises a difficulty which has almost uniformly been resolved by printing the textus in a smaller type than the MS: this not only makes for "stripy" looking pages, but also ensures that the textus will probably not be read as attentively as is needed to give substance to the MS note. Mr. Richard Garnett, designer of the *Collected Coleridge* volumes, after carefully considering various alternatives, decided to print the textus in the same size of type as the MS and to print the MS in a second colour — a device (if you can afford it) that makes the primary Coleridge text instantly recognisable yet lightens the visual emphasis on the MS to correspond approximately to the visual effect of the original annotated volumes; it also provides a ready means of showing clearly Coleridge's own corrections and alterations to the textus.

As in the Coleridge *Notebooks* (but unlike the Coleridge *Letters*) I am printing a *literatim* transcript of the manuscript notes — with peculiarities of spelling and punctuation, slips of the pen, unintentional duplication of words, all cancelled words and passages (as far as possible) restored, and the Greek pointed or not pointed according to Coleridge's variable practice. In the printed text however these slips and idiosyncrasies will not be signalled by "[*sic*]" or "[!]," on the assumption that the text will in the end be so accurately printed that the reader can take it that whatever oddity is in the printed text was in fact in the MS. When transcribing textus I have also decided (contrary to HNC's practice) to follow the typographical idiosyncrasies of the particular edition that Coleridge was using. He wrote notes on books of every period from the fifteenth century to the date of his death; he has a reasonable eye for typography and is aware of the changes in sensation that occur if the book is beautifully printed (as some of his were), or if the type is roughly devised, or if the text bristles with capitals and is (as the Cambridge Press has it) "hirsute with commas." He is aware whether he is reading a quarto in the manner of Baskerville or Bodoni, or a little Elzevir to stuff in a pocket, or a contemporary sermonising octavo in which the type no more holds the eye than the enervating tone holds the attention. It is not possible now to reproduce the beautiful Greek types that delighted him in the copy of Arrian given him as an Indian gift in Syracuse by Stoddart, and even if we could it is unlikely that many these days would be able to read it with ease; and it is not reasonable to cut special characters for the two Greek digraphs that he commonly used for *st-* and *ou-* or to reproduce the ligatures and suspensions common in some early founts and some versions of Fraktur. The line has to be drawn somewhere; but as far as the normal range of a Monotype matrix-frame will allow, the typographical texture of the printed original will be honoured. When the textus is in a language other than English, a translation is provided, together with the original.

Coleridge's hand is normally not difficult to read with reasonable confidence. Admittedly from time to time it is *not* written normally, and the cramped position of the book, the constriction of space when he still has more to say, or the misbehaviour of a hastily cut reed or quill, or the fine ink-spattering of a steel pen catching the chain-lines on a rough-surfaced laid paper will do things to the writing that give a transcriber pause. In general the main difficulties in establishing a good text arise, not so much from Coleridge's handwriting (which on the whole – *pace* Charles Lamb – is workmanlike and distinct), but from the physical damage that the notes have suffered since they were written – damage that had already started to occur while Coleridge was still using and annotating some of the books. This is of two kinds: the decay of pencil marks, and the cropping of margins. Coleridge's pencils seem always to have been soft and not to have made a good black mark. In his German books, because of the *papyrus cacatoria* (in which phrase he distorts Catullus almost as much as the paper disfigures his writing), he had to choose between writing on the text in pencil or writing in ink on flyleaves. He often did both; and the pencil marks are in many cases now sadly rubbed and faded, and, after 150 years of standing in bookcases with the leaves tightly pressed together, the notes are overset page upon page in a ghostly and tantalizing confusion. Although Coleridge did not follow Lamb in inflicting upon his favourite books a process of accelerated decay – with wine-stains, tobacco ash, and crumbs of cheese and bread (I have never found snuff) – many of his books (which he often bought in a condition far from mint) wore out from

Coleridge note in pencil on Schelling

F. W. J. Schelling, *Philosophische Schriften*, vol. I
(Landshut, 1809), p. 2

Part of one of 70 notes written in this volume between
1812 and 1815. The paper, as usual in Coleridge's German
books, induced him to write in pencil; confusion at the
foot comes from the offsetting of the rest of the note on
the facing page. The leaves are cropped., with severe loss at
the foot; but Coleridge wrote notes in this volume after
"The Book-binder [had] docked my former notes."
(British Museum C.126.g.7; reproduced by permission of
the Trustees.)

Wissens — zugleich als Urgrund aller Realität herr-
schen.

Giebt es überhaupt ein Wissen, so muss es ein
Wissen geben, zu dem ich nicht wieder durch ein
anders Wissen gelange, und durch welches allein alles andre Wissen Wissen ist. Wir brauchen nicht
ein besondre Art von Wissen vorauszusetzen, um zu
diesem Satze zu gelangen. Wenn wir nur überhaupt
etwas wissen, so müssen wir auch Eines wenigstens
wissen, zu dem wir nicht wieder durch ein andres
Wissen gelangen, und das selbst den Realgrund alles
unsers Wissens enthält.

Dieses Letzte im menschlichen Wissen kann also
seinen Realgrund nicht wieder in etwas anderem
suchen müssen, es ist nicht nur selbst unabhängig
von irgend etwas Höherem, sondern, da unser Wissen nur von der Folge zum Grund aufsteigt, und
umgekehrt vom Grund zur Folge fortschreitet, muss
auch das, was das Höchste, und für uns Princip
alles Erkennens ist, nicht wieder durch ein anders
Princip erkennbar seyn, d. h. das Princip seines
Seyns und das Princip seines Erkennens muss zu-
sammenfallen, muss Eines seyn, denn nur, weil es
selbst, nicht weil irgend etwas anders ist, kann es
gedacht werden. Es muss also gedacht werden, nur
weil es ist, und es muss seyn, nicht weil irgend etwas anders, sondern weil es selbst gedacht wird:
sein Bejahen muss in seinem Denken enthalten seyn,
es muss sich durch sein Denken selbst hervorbringen.
Müsste man, um zu seinem Denken zu gelangen, ein andres denken, so wäre dieses höher
als das Höchste, das sich widerspricht: um zum
Höchsten zu gelangen, brauche ich nichts, als dieses

repeated use and had to be rebound either by himself or
later by his literary executor and members of his family;
the German books, normally issued in paper wrappers,
suffered particularly; some of Coleriedge's instructions to
the binder — not always scrupulously followed — are still
to be seen in these books: and in his rebound copy of
Schelling's *Philosophische Schriften* he has noted — "The
Book-binder has docked my former notes, but I understand enough to find that my first impressions were the
same as my present one." And sometimes in rebinding,
flyleaves and wrappers, preserved for what was written on
them, have been jumbled out of their original order and
even separated from their original volumes. For an
annotated book to be rebound is usually a disaster. Ever
since the invention of printing, binders have had a
notoriously heavy hand with the guillotine. Preoccupied
with externals — leather and tooling, marbled paper and
coloured paste — they indulge the ruthless love of clean
surfaces that is often ascribed to neurotic housewives.
Sometimes the owner of an annotated book will have given
his binder strict injunction to withhold the knife, or — not
trusting the binder — will have folded in the annotated
margins to withdraw them from the cutting edge. But
there are a sad number of Coleridge's annotated books that
can no longer be described as "opened but uncut." When a
note in an outer margin is cropped the text can often be
restored with some confidence — given an ear for
Coleridge's prose and a more than superficial acquaintance
with his enormous vocabulary and his habit of coining
words when no existing word will serve his purpose. But
notes that have crowded into the last millimetre of a head-
or foot-margin can suffer irremediable loss, and only rarely
will a scatter of the tops of ascenders survive to tempt the
editor into supposing that by some act of intuitive grace or
cryptographic inspiration he will be able to recover just one
more line of manuscript.

In a few cases — but not nearly as many as one could
wish — one of the early editors transcribed the notes

before the guillotine fell; for there are preserved at Victoria College a quantity of the working papers of Henry Nelson Coleridge and Sara, and of Ernest Hartley Coleridge. These MS TRANSCRIPTS will sometimes provide a middle position between the original notes in a book now lost and the printed text of those notes; where it is clear that the printed text has moved away from the original through normalisation or stylistic revision, the MS TRANSCRIPT is taken as the best authority. In several cases the transcripts were not printed, and now provide the only witness to the notes written in books now lost.

At the outset I had hoped to arrange the marginalia in chronological order, in the way the notebook entries are arranged. The difficulties have in the end proved insuperable. Although there is not usually much difficulty in putting a plausible date to a reading of a book or to a group of marginalia, it is clear that many books have been read and reread, and annotated on several occasions, sometimes with notes on his own notes; and in some other cases, often in books that are not heavily annotated, it is impossible to say with certainty that all the notes were written at one time. Alternations between ink and pencil, and changes in the handwriting itself, seldom provide conclusive evidence for dating. To pretend to be able to ascribe every one of the 177 notes on Boehme definitely to one of the five or six "readings" that occurred over fifteen years would be to claim a certainty that the evidence will not support. As far as possible I have separated out the chronological layers of notes in each book, but with an acute sense of the vagueness of the penumbral areas of judgment in such matters and the way conjecture linked to conjecture can breed a monster. But this separation is confined to the description in the headnote to an entry; in all cases the notes are printed in a single sequence as though they had been written at a single reading.

For a time I considered whether a topical arrangement could be followed — as HNC and Sara intended — grouping literary, theological, and political notes, and adding the philosophical, biblical, and scientific notes that fell outside their scheme. This proposal looks so reasonable and manageable that it could be expected *not* to serve the Coleridge materials. It is one thing for a librarian to place a book in a subject category, deciding for example that Defoe's *History of the Plague Year* is fiction and not history; it is quite another — as any indexer of Coleridge's work knows — to categorize a Coleridge *note*, and yet another to categorize a *series* of marginal notes on a single book. For example, the marginalia on Marcus Aurelius's *Meditations* (translated by Jeremy Collier, London 1701) are 68 in number (not counting about 75 passages marked mostly by way of stylistic comment); they were written in two series — about 27 notes January to May 1804 in London and at sea on the voyage to Malta, and the rest January to June 1808 in London after his return and perhaps also at Bury St. Edmunds. Many of the early notes deal with prose style: when he started reading the book he was impressed more by the "slang and ribaldry" of Collier's style than by the noble if confused stoicism of Marcus Aurelius that could have provided a thread to lead him back into the labyrinthine spaces of his beloved Heraclitus. There are also in the marginalia on Marcus Aurelius notes on Burns's poetry, on Andrew Bell's educational theory, on the characteristic differences between various languages, on Sir Robert Walpole and Sir George Beaumont, on prophecy, on Dr. Thomas Beddoes; there is a recollection of his own father's sudden death and a dream that presaged it; and notes on the relation between soul and body, on love and marriage, fame and reputation, on John Donne's book on suicide called *Biathanatos*, on Isaac Barrow's sermons, on the distinction between man and brutes, and on the soul as a glow-worm; a cluster of personal images brings together butterflies, fire (Heraclitan), and a recurrent pun on *Son* and *Sun*; there are notes on Quakers, Lord Nelson, chemical terminology and Humphry Davy, a recollection of the Salutation and

Cat with Lamb and a sly nip at Leibniz and Newton as students of alchemy. To place this set of marginalia in the category of "Philosophy, Stoic" with a cross-reference to Heraclitus would catch rather less than a quarter of the notes even if the classificatory principle were stretched to its most generous limit; and it would do less than justice to the rest, or simply bury them; and anyway Marcus Aurelius's *Meditations* is not where one would normally look for a note on the possibility that Davy's most recent chemical discoveries might provide a new nomenclature for psychology. The Aurelius notes are not entirely typical of all the marginalia; yet they are not entirely atypical either – as a glance through the notebooks in their chronological arrangement will show, or Keats's brilliant but accurate record of what unfolded in Coleridge's monologue in the course of a single walk over Hampstead Heath. Any serious attempt to place the *marginalia* (rather than the books) in topical arrangement would (I suspect) lead to even more serious and misleading dislocations than an attempt at chronological arrangement. Topical questions will have to be answered through a careful index; and the chronology can be seen, at least in broad outline, through a list showing what books were being annotated year by year.

For the marginalia themselves I have decided upon an alphabetical arrangement by author – aware though I am of Coleridge's distaste for the arbitrariness of alphabetical arrangement. This comes less as a counsel of despair than with the conviction that it will not do violence to the integrity of separate series of notes and that it may well convey something of the vivid and manifold activity of this "myriad-minded man." Certainly it produces some strange bedfellows, neighbours, and crocodiles. William Blake is followed by Joseph Blanco White (Spanish Jesuit turned ambitious Anglican controversialist), then William Blomfield (Bishop of London), then Blumenbach (the celebrated naturalist whose lectures Coleridge attended at Göttingen and never forgot), then Boccaccio (about whom he had some misgivings), Jacob Boehme (theosophic

mystic), Boerhaave (Dutch chemist); and the forged
Memoirs of the Count de Bonneval (a life scabrous and
sensational enough if truly told) are followed by *The Book
of Common Prayer*. Another sequence runs: Philip de
Commines, Barry Cornwall, Abraham Cowley, Oliver
Cromwell, Dallison (author of a Caroline tract), the *Dance
of Death*; then we have – Samuel Daniel and, after Dante,
Alexander Charles Louis d'Arblay, son of Fanny Burney
and the fugitive General d'Arblay, who presents Coleridge
with a copy of a funeral sermon on the death of George IV
inscribed "From one of the humblest admirers of his
genius." Eichhorn the Biblical neologist lies next to the
Eikon Basilike; Fichte and Ficino are next door neighbours; Goldfuss (the Schellingian chemist) stands on one
side of Thomas Gray, and Fulke Greville, Lord Brooke, on
the other; Bernard Mandeville's *Fable of the Bees* is
followed by Cotton Mather's *Magnalia Christi Americana*;
Milton is followed by Henry More, Thomas More, and a
pathetic refugee with the improbable name of Cesare
Mussolini; Napoleon is followed by Nemesius; Samuel Parr
goes before Pascal; Thomas Pringle (the first librarian at
Cape Town and later secretary to the Anti-Slavery Society)
is followed by Proclus; Rabelais, Raleigh, and Randolph go
hand in hand; Robert Southey is flanked by William
Sotheby and Benedict Spinoza; and the alphabet trails off
with Swedenborg, Swift, Swinburne, Jeremy Taylor, Tenn-
yson, Valckenaer . . . and ends with three Wordsworths,
Francis Wrangham, Xenophon, the *Zeitschrift für Specula-
tive Physik*, and Zwick. And since this is an alphabetical
list, not of Coleridge's library, but of the books he wrote
marginalia in, these constellations are no more accidental
and no less felicitous than the first three subject entries for
the London Library: acrobatics, aeronautics, aesthetics.
For Coleridge's profound sense of the unity of thought, of
the past living in the present, allows him to move from
Heironymus Fracastorius to the youthful Alfred Tenny-
son, or from Paracelsus to Jeremy Taylor, and read them
all in much the same way, the authors present to him,

himself listening for the hound-voices that declare the mind's affectionate and strenuous penetration into the dark adyta of human life and the intricacies of the universe. Perhaps at some later date the breath of Baconian – or Coleridgean – method may inspire somebody to articulate these writings into a different and more organic form. For the time being the alphabetical arrangement is nothing if not suggestive; and for myself, for the moment, I am content with it.

SOURCES AND LOCATION

When an editor has his text before him, then properly speaking his editorial work begins – to prepare a text that is accurate, complete, and if possible capable of going on its own feet. I must confess to have smudged a little the purity of the editorial art by engaging in certain exploratory and detective activities in trying to determine with some accuracy the limits of an ideally inclusive text. I felt it necessary to reconstruct as best I could the contents of Coleridge's library, the way it grew, what books he had with him at certain times, and where and when he left books behind. Beyond possession there is the generosity of friends – as Lamb memorably observed with a drop or two of tungstic acid; so it was necessary to find out what books he borrowed from libraries and from his friends – and if possible when, if ever, he returned them; and since the history of his library and of his reading is not quite the same as the history of his marginalia, to determine why he wrote marginalia at all, for whom, and under what conditions both mental and physical.

The way of doing these things is in general familiar enough to any literary scholar; yet I may be allowed to reflect a little upon the way of doing this in Coleridge's case. This brings me back to my second motto, about first catching the hare. What hare? The first stage was to identify all published marginalia, in the posthumous editions, in periodicals, and elsewhere; to compile a list of association books and their locations; to set up a spider's

web of the history of Coleridge's reading, based on his own
writing, published and in manuscript. No doubt every such
task has its own peculiar characteristics. In my own case I
happened to have to wait almost three years before seeing
many annotated books; and when I did get at the
annotated books — first at Harvard, then in the British
Museum — I found the undertaking changing greatly in
scope and in subtlety of implication. Perhaps the physical
nature of the materials has much to do with the tone of
any editorial activity; and (again fortunately) since at that
time there was no xerox, photography was beyond my
means, and microfilm an abomination, I was obliged to
work almost entirely from originals. (Even now, because of
the state of the books or the notes themselves, that is still
largely the case.) And fortunately the place this had to be
done was that most glorious of all libraries, the British
Museum. The North Library in those days was an
enchanted place, discreet and undemocratic, where a
privileged reader had his name displayed at his desk and
ordinary books and papers could be left there from day to
day. If in the early post-war years there were times in the
unheated library when the fog would miserably invade
Smirke's great dome and it was well to wear a greatcoat
and shooting mits, and the early winter darkness as you
came down the steps at the end of the day had a
Beowulf-ish frisson to it or the iron taste of a middle
watch off Cape Wrath — all this mattered too; at least the
North Library was not the North Sea, and one lay to an
anchor at the heart of the greatest public collection of
Coleridgeana in the world, with access to the unfathom-
able collections that seem to be needed to unstitch
Coleridge's writing. Here indeed the spider's web assumed
a new density, not only from the original books and
manuscripts but from the resources that it seems to take
half a lifetime to find out how to use.

Here, for example, I first came across several of the "MS
FACSIMILES," a few in the central collection, but mostly
in the Ashley Library. These are not forgeries, but copies

of Coleridge's notes, usually made by or for the Gillmans
by transcribing sets of notes into copies of the editions the
original notes were written in. Wise had plenty of genuine
examples of Coleridge's hand in his collection, but he so
often saw what he wanted to see that he described some of
these MS FACSIMILES in the *Ashley Catalogue* in great
detail, as though they were originals, with reproductions to
illustrate his alleged point, and on one occasion expatiating
upon the quality of Coleridge's handwriting when it was
obviously somebody else's. In some cases, not many, a MS
FACSIMILE is the only record we have of certain
marginalia, so identification of the transcribers is important if possible. It is well that there are so few; for a
comparison of (say) Field's *Of the Church* or Donne's
Poems with the original marginalia shows serious lapses in
accuracy, many misreadings, an inability to read Greek and
to write it; and when the notes are copious they are
usually overtaken by the same fatigue that afflicts even the
hand-rubricated capitals in the later pages of Coleridge's
one incunable.

Another discovery – for me, that is – was the auction
sale catalogues. Although it was David Foxon (then on the
BM staff) who taught me as much about how to use the
British Museum library as he did about how to eat well
within a cock's stride of the museum, I distinctly
remember that it was Kathleen Coburn who first showed
me the sale catalogue of J. H. Green's library, the source
for most of the BM's original collection of annotated
books and for most of the Coleridgeana in the U.S. The
BM's holdings of auction sale catalogues is peculiarly
valuable, for most of them are the auctioneer's copies,
showing in MS the prices paid, and the buyers' names, and
occasionally a substantial revision to the description of a
catalogued item. By examining a number of these, the web
established by plotting the history of Coleridge's reading
took on another dimension: certain nodes appeared in the
process of dispersal, the patterns of dispersal began to
emerge, and search areas were much more clearly defined.

The catalogues also identified annotated books previously unknown, or gave substance to certain shadowy possibilities that peeped out from Coleridge's writing. In a few cases I was able to locate private collections, happily to find that the owners who had cherished the books for personal or family reasons were unaware of the interest and value of those books. When John Hayward invited me to contribute to the *Book Collector* something on Coleridge under the general title of "Portrait of a Bibliophile," I smuggled in an account of the collection and dispersal of Coleridge's books. And because I love graphs and diagrams I contrived a single diagram to illustrate the lines of accumulation and dispersal from c. 1805 to 1961. It was ingenious certainly; I thought it rather elegant, and was saddened when he blue-pencilled it. "I really couldn't print that," he said, "it looks like a piece of plumbing" – and after a moment's reflection – "or like a sketch for one of Vesalius's more intimate anatomical drawings." There were still chaste sensibilities in those days. I am sure my diagram will not be published in the *Collected Coleridge* and if I don't destroy it, it may remain like one of those Egyptian cats that look out wistfully from their mummy-cloths to perplex some fifth-generation archaeologist.

To define the outer limits of an ideal text made it possible to define the actual text; and I decided to make two exclusions from what had originally been a complete Reading List: (a) annotated copies of his own works – these to go to the editors of separate works in the *Collected Coleridge*; and (b) "Marked Books," which would be described in an Appendix. To be able to reconstruct (to some extent) Coleridge's library, the libraries of his friends, and the patterns of accumulation and dispersal gave greater precision to one's guesses about interlocking biographical evidence. There are always *lacrimabiles lacunae* – of these the destruction of Charles Lamb's library, almost without record, is the most lamentable. Fortunately Mrs. Green made a handlist of 237 annotated and marked books, apparently after J. H.

Green's death, sketchy and incomplete (otherwise the Green Sale of 1880 would not have stocked the BM and a few U.S. libraries with Coleridge's books as it did); one member of the Gillman family made a short list, and family correspondence has recovered a few others. But the handlist of the Rydal Hall library is of greater importance than any of these, not only for the more than 300 Coleridge titles, some of them otherwise unrecorded, but also for the terminal dates it allows us to place on certain of these books for Coleridge's use. The evidence of sale catalogues and library catalogues has also, in unexpected ways, thrown light on the actual relations between Coleridge and Wordsworth, Lamb, Sara Hutchinson, Robert Southey, Thomas De Quincey.

Having identified the books and located as many as possible, and patched up the gaps in the text from whatever reliable sources present themselves, there are still two more phases to be encompassed. One is dating, the other is providing footnotes.

DATING

Although I had decided long ago that a chronological arrangement of the marginalia would be misleading, even if possible, it is still necessary to put a date on the marginalia written in each book. In some cases the marginalia pretty clearly were written at one stride; but in many others they were written in layers, often in several layers; and the layers are characteristically disposed in a horizontal sense, interleaved in a succession of readings rather than accumulated in the book part by part. Coleridge seldom dates his marginalia, but sometimes a postscript or a note on a note will be dated; the intervals are sometimes 20 years or more. The date of acquisition is by no means always a certain indication of the date of the notes. And if at one end of the scale certain notes present no difficulty to date, at the other end dating may involve a most delicate weighing of complex evidence, both internal and external — biographical, historical, bibliographical, topical. The imprint and the *English Catalogue* sometimes provide a useful terminus. To know *whose* book it was is always a help, and the published *Notebooks* and *Letters* will sometimes provide evidence that keys into the marginalia with a plausible air of finality. As is to be expected, the writing of his friends provides hints and clues; and internal evidence (say of Davy's knighthood, or Beddoes's death, of Katterfelto's black cats, or the known date of first acquaintance with a book or author) sometimes helps to separate layers of notes. And beyond these, Coleridge's changing attitude to certain individuals and books and ideas will provide a clue; or the spelling of a name, or the use of a steel pen or red chalk, certain kinds of slips in German or Italian, the pointing of the Greek, a minute argument involving Hebrew with an assurance scarcely possible before the meeting with Hyman Hurwitz. General habits and uses of marginal annotation can be detected; and at times one can feel the *presence* of the person the notes were written for. But Coleridge is mercurial as well as protean. These complexities of evidence need to be handled very warily and with a light hand, for the possibilities of cumulative plausible error — arising from an overemphatic use of any kind of evidence — are indeed formidable. For we are dealing with a mind "capacious and systematizing," with a man with a remarkable capacity for precise verbal recall; and he often writes (as he said of the notebooks) "more unconscious that I am writing, than in my most earnest modes I *talk*." One would not expect to find in the marginalia on Jacob Boehme, for example, both a draft for the closing paragraph of the *Biographia Literaria*, and a hitherto unrecorded version of the hexameters he wrote to the Wordsworths in Germany in 1799. Yet the first was written apparently in 1809 or 1810, and the second certainly in 1822.

FOOTNOTING

Coleridge can write notes on notes whenever he wishes, and as editors we must deal with them as primary text. But

when an editor writes notes on Coleridge's notes − notes
that he says were often "cogitabilia rather than cogitata a
me" − he needs a sense of propriety, tact, and courage. The
fact is that Coleridge is immensely learned, and most of all
he knows at any time is continuously at his disposal. In
most of the marginalia − that is, in all the marginalia not
specifically written for somebody else (and even in some
of those) − he is writing in much the same swift, nervous,
deft manner as he writes in the notebooks. The writing is a
little less intimate, less private than in the notebooks, yet
it has the same characteristic fluent and shapely coherence,
even when most trenchant; for no matter how impacted
the writing may be, no matter how set about with
cantilevered parentheses, and often elliptical to our eye, it
is not shorthand, and it does not confront us with private
puzzles to be deciphered. It all made clear sense to him. It
is as though he were himself overhearing what he is in the
act of saying. For semantic obscurities and for identifica-
tions, and even for foreign languages, the editor has a clear
duty to provide information − information that Coleridge
usually, in more or less precise form, had in his own head.
The extent of information we need to provide in order to
recapture the quotidian content of Coleridge's mind,
however, seems to broaden almost daily as the literacy of
the West "dissolves, diffuses, and dissipates" without much
prospect of ever reconstituting the coherent unity that it
had for Coleridge and many of his contemporaries. But
beyond providing information (which one always hopes
will not offend anybody who already has it), the annotator
needs to assume − and allow the reader somehow to
assume − the ambience of Coleridge's thinking and feeling.
Theoretically the primary text can do that, but I am not
always confident that many readers will in all cases find
that the text *is* self-evident.

Footnoting of the less commendable sort that one has
seen in published editions can range from hectoring
verbosity and importunate pedantry to the complete
silence that comes not from restraint, but from cowardice

or apathy. This will not do for Coleridge. What Coleridge
clearly demands from time to time is not interpretation
and explanation, but elucidation – the releasing of the
text to take flight in its own way or to creep along the
ground if it wishes. Depending on the demands of the text
and the tact of the editor, the footnotes may usually be
terse and pointed; but sometimes they need to be rendered
in patient – even opulent – detail. Fidelity to the text is a
virtue we all recognise as essential; and beyond fidelity
there is (or so Coleridge persuades me) "truth to the text,"
saying what needs to be said about the ambience of a
thought, its resonances, its initiative, its constituent
physique perhaps, its implied universe. There is a text
given, and it is Coleridge who wrote it; no matter how
illegible or crabbed or dense, the text must be allowed to
stand forth in its *own* light. Although we cannot encom-
pass all Coleridge's learning or the whole sweep of his mind
and imagination, we can enter into it; and in doing so it is
well that we set down what by whatever means we happen
to know belongs to it. In being positively true to the text,
the emergent tone of the edition is (I suppose) of
importance; agility, modesty, delight; and the delineation
needs to be firm but never preclusive (unless it be matter
of demonstrable fact), suggestive rather than definitive,
illuminating in a way that allows the primary text to well
up and grow in the reader's mind as it did in Coleridge's, at
once new and familiar. For an editor's text is his privilege,
not his property.

And in the end, sometime, the great machines of
editorial industry and erudition will be able to run down,
the first tasks finished. Then there can come forth clean
companionable texts, as pretty to look at as Ernest Hartley
Coleridge's *Anima Poetae* and as unobtrusive in their
wisdom as *Inquiring Spirit*, the notes and preliminary aids
having slipped away into the humus of learned discourse to
nourish what they may and inform as they can. Coleridge
once said that he followed the chamois-hunters and loved
the effort and dangers of the chase; but that if he hunted

well – and it wasn't even metaphorical chamois-goats he was hunting – others would be able to walk a highway thereafter or enjoy the view, with no need to take "desperate Leaps and Balloons that soar indeed but do not improve the chances of getting forward." If as editors we are rock-climbers attempting the North Face of the Eiger, we need to be sure that the gossamers and filaments we leave on the Hinterstoisser Traverse will stand the weather; and if we wish to prepare a way that others may travel without too much effort or danger we need to be sure that the exhilaration of the first journey is not dissipated, that the high altitudes and high latitudes and the swamps and jungles and the quiet villages have not turned banal through our reports of what we have seen there. I reckon myself fortunate to have come upon Coleridge's mind, so perpetual a cause for wonder and source of refreshment; fortunate too to share in this hazard with some resolute and high-spirited rock-climbers, friends and colleagues whose minds are invigorated by the enterprise, their vision armed, their temper sweetened as much by the quality of the task as by its magnitude.

The disposition and dispersal of Coleridge's Library, 1800-1970 (redrawn from the author's original sketch; see above, p. 111).

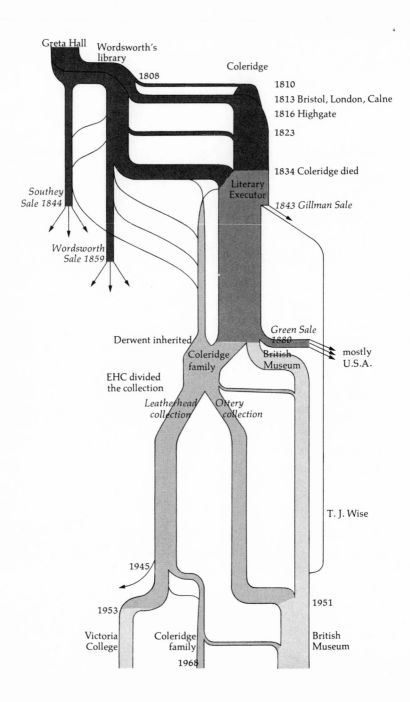

Greta Hall Wordsworth's
library

1808

Coleridge

1810

1813 Bristol, London, Calne

1816 Highgate

1823

1834 Coleridge died

Literary
Executor

1843 Gillman Sale

*Southey
Sale 1844*

*Wordsworth
Sale 1859*

*Green Sale
1880*

Derwent inherited

Coleridge
family

British
Museum

mostly
U.S.A.

EHC divided
the collection

*Leatherhead
collection*

*Ottery
collection*

T. J. Wise

1945

1951

1953

Victoria
College

Coleridge
family

British
Museum

1968

Members of the Conference

Thomas L. Ashton, *University of Massachusetts*
John D. Baird, *Victoria College, University of Toronto*
G. E. Bentley, Jr., *University College, University of Toronto*
Kenneth Blackwell, *Bertrand Russell Archives, McMaster University*
W. F. Blissett, *University College, University of Toronto*
J. H. Burns, *University College London*
J. E. Chamberlin, *University College, University of Toronto*
W. C. Chau, *Ryerson Polytechnical Institute*
Kathleen Coburn, *Victoria College, University of Toronto*
Beatrice Corrigan, *University of Toronto*
Jared R. Curtis, *Simon Fraser University*
H. B. de Groot, *University College, University of Toronto*
Harold O. Dendurent, *University of Maine*
A. H. de Quehen, *University College, University of Toronto*
Donald D. Eddy, *Cornell University*

M. S. Elliott, *York University*
David G. Esplin, *University of Toronto Library*
P. D. Fleck, *University of Western Ontario*
Marilyn Gaull, *Temple University*
James M. Good, *University of Western Ontario*
Francess G. Halpenny, *Dictionary of Canadian Biography, University of Toronto Press*
Cyrus Hamlin, *Victoria College, University of Toronto*
Joyce Hemlow, *McGill University*
Patricia Hernlund, *Wayne State University*
Marian J. Horn, *University of Toronto Library*
James A. Houck, *Youngstown State University*
Roderick Huang, *University of Windsor*
Mr. and Mrs. J. R. de J. Jackson, *Victoria College, University of Toronto*
Jean C. Jamieson, *University of Toronto Press*
B. W. Jones, *Carleton University*
W. B. Lambert, *University of Lethbridge*
C. L. Lambertson, *University of Victoria*
Richard N. Lutes, *Wayne State University*
James R. MacGillivray, *University of Toronto*
N. Mackenzie, *Ryerson Polytechnical Institute*
Kenneth MacLean, *Victoria College, University of Toronto*
John McClelland, *Victoria College, University of Toronto*
George F. McFarland, *St. Lawrence University*
Peter Moes, *Scarborough College, University of Toronto*
Mr. and Mrs. Peter F. Morgan, *University College, University of Toronto*
Rev. James P. Morro, *Pontifical Institute of Medieval Studies*
W. J. B. Owen, *McMaster University*
Sybille Pantazzi, *Art Gallery of Ontario*
Donald G. Priestman, *Ryerson Polytechnical Institute*
Donald H. Reiman, *The Carl H. Pforzheimer Library*
Dr. and Mrs. Thomas A. Reisner, *Laval University*

John G. Rideout, *Lakehead University*
F. W. Roberts, *University of Texas at Austin*
Derek V. Robertson, *Mills Memorial Library, McMaster University*
John M. Robson, *Victoria College, University of Toronto*
Barbara E. Rooke, *Trent University*
Ann Saddlemyer, *Victoria College, University of Toronto*
W. D. Shaw, *Victoria College, University of Toronto*
J. M. Stedmond, *Queen's University*
Thomas E. Tausky, *University of Western Ontario*
Prudence Tracy, *University of Toronto Press*
Elizabeth M. Vida, *University of Saskatchewan*
Edward Watson, *University of Windsor*
George Whalley, *Queen's University*
L. H. Willis, *University of Guelph*
Gail Wilson, *University of Toronto Library*
Jean Wilson, *University of Toronto Press*
Milton Wilson, *Trinity College, University of Toronto*
Dorothy E. Zaborszky, *Laurentian University*

Index